MW01043320

46394

Plaistow Public Library

PLAISTOW PUBLIC LIBRARY
14 ELM ST. P.O. BOX 186
PLAISTOW, N.H. 03865

GAYLORD R

COMMUNITIES
OF THE
Faithful

J 291.9 AND

TRICIA ANDRYSZEWSKI

COMMUNITIES
OF THE
Faithful
AMERICAN
RELIGIOUS MOVEMENTS
OUTSIDE
THE MAINSTREAM

PLAISTOW PUBLIC LIBRARY
14 ELM ST. P.O. BOX 186
PLAISTOW, N.H. 03865

The Millbrook Press
Brookfield, Connecticut

Cover photograph courtesy of William Strode/SuperStock

Photographs courtesy of © Renato Rotolo/Gamma Liaison: pp.14, 21;
© Mark Ludak, Impact Visuals: p. 24; Hancock Shaker Village, Pittsfield,
Massachusetts: pp. 28, 31, 34; © Richard Elkins/Gamma Liaison: p. 42;
National Portrait Gallery, Smithsonian Institution/Art Resource, NY:
p. 47; Bettmann: pp. 54, 70, 75, 93; Marquette University Archives: pp.
57, 62; © Bob Fitch/Black Star: p. 67; © Douglas Burrows/Gamma
Liaison: p. 81; © Carol Halebian/Gamma Liaison: p. 86; © Clark Jones,
Impact Visuals: p. 96; Bequest of Maxim Karolik, Museum of Fine Arts,
Boston: p. 101; Friends Historical Library of Swarthmore College,
Swarthmore, Pennsylvania: p. 106; American Friends Service Committee
Archives: p. 109.

Published in 1997 by The Millbrook Press, Inc.
2 Old New Milford Road
Brookfield, Connecticut 06804

Copyright © 1997 by Tricia Andryszewski
All rights reserved
Printed in the United States of America
1 3 5 4 2

Library of Congress Cataloging-in-Publication Data
Andryszewski,Tricia, 1956-
Communities of the Faithful: American religious movements outside the
mainstream/Tricia Andryszewski.
p.   cm.
Includes bibliographical references and index.
Summary: Explores seven distinctive American religious communities
which derived from Judaism, Christianity, or Islam; included are Amish,
Shakers, Mormons, Catholic Workers, Nation of Islam, Lubavitcher
Hasidim, and Quakers.
ISBN 0-7613-0067-8 (lib. bdg.)
1. Sects--United States—Juvenile literature. 2. Cults—United States—
Juvenile literature. 3. United States—Religion--1960- [1. Sects. 2. Cults.
3. Religions.] I. Title.
BL2525.A566   1997
291.9'0973—dc21   97-1385   CIP   AC

CONTENTS

Foreword
11

Old Order Amish
15

Shakers
27

Mormons
41

Catholic Workers
56

Nation of Islam
71

Lubavitcher Hasidim
85

Quakers
100

Notes   115
Index   121

"YOU ARE THE SALT OF THE EARTH; BUT IF THE SALT LOSES
ITS STRENGTH, WHAT SHALL IT BE SALTED WITH?"
—MATTHEW 5:13, NEW CATHOLIC EDITION

COMMUNITIES
OF THE
Faithful

FOREWORD

This book tells the stories of seven distinctive American religious communities. Derived from the three great Western parent religions—Judaism, Christianity, and Islam—these seven only hint at the astonishing diversity of American religious life.

There's no treatment of conventional Catholicism here, nor of the mainstream Protestant, Jewish, or Islamic denominations. Nor will we look at Native American beliefs or at American representatives of Eastern faiths.

Instead, here are seven communities that stand out from the mainstream, but whose values and religious traditions overlap with those of more familiar religious organizations. Some of the seven started overseas and later established themselves in America; others arose in the United States. All have developed distinctively American identities, and all have made unique contributions to American life.

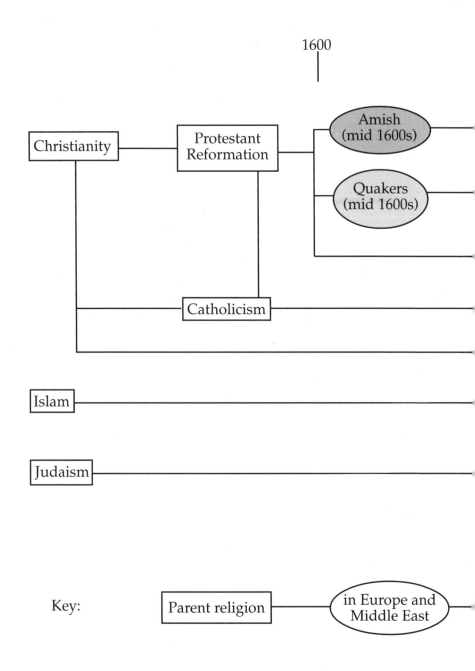

1600

Christianity

Protestant Reformation

Amish (mid 1600s)

Quakers (mid 1600s)

Catholicism

Islam

Judaism

Key:

Parent religion

in Europe and Middle East

(12)

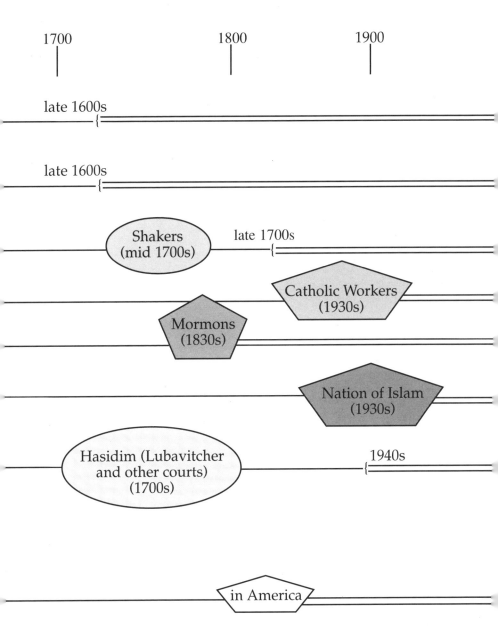

1700   1800   1900

late 1600s

late 1600s

Shakers
(mid 1700s)   late 1700s

Catholic Workers
(1930s)

Mormons
(1830s)

Nation of Islam
(1930s)

Hasidim (Lubavitcher
and other courts)
(1700s)   1940s

in America

An Amish farm in Pennsylvania looks tranquil in the early morning light. The farm and the family are at the center of Amish life.

OLD ORDER AMISH

"THE LAND IS GOD'S. IT'S MY JOB, AND THE JOB OF
EVERY AMISH PERSON, TO TAKE CARE OF IT FOR HIM.
WE MUSTN'T TRY TO CHANGE OR CONQUER NATURE
OR EXPLOIT THE LAND. THAT WOULD BE GOING
AGAINST GOD'S WAY."

— AN AMISH MAN[1]

For three centuries, the Old Order Amish in America
have been following the simple lifestyle they consider "God's way." Their large colony near
Lancaster, Pennsylvania, has grown despite losing
members to the temptations of modern life in the
"outside" world. It may yet be destroyed, however,
by its own growth.

The Amish in America

The Amish were part of a larger group of Protestants,
the Anabaptists, who came to America beginning in
the late 1600s from the region of Europe near where
the borders of Switzerland, Germany, and France

now meet. Anabaptists generally were radical reformers favoring a strictly disciplined Christian community made up of consenting adults (only adults could be baptized) and a more equitable social order reflecting everyone's equality before God. In Europe they were cruelly persecuted for their beliefs. The Amish branch of Anabaptism followed the distinctive teachings of Jacob Amman, which included having the congregation take communion twice a year, and meeting for Sunday worship in members' homes rather than in a church.

The first Amish immigrants settled in eastern Pennsylvania. Other Amish communities eventually established themselves throughout the Northeast and Midwest, and in Canada. Today, the vast majority of Amish communities are located in Ohio, Pennsylvania, and Indiana.

The Amish govern themselves as separate communities. Although like-minded communities do keep in touch with one another, there is no overall authority that codifies their beliefs or enforces the rules for Amish life. As a result, over the years different communities have developed differently. (Communities that agree with one another on all important points are said to be "in full fellowship" with one another, and their members are permitted to intermingle freely.) Some communities have merged with branches of the Mennonite church, also descended from Anabaptism. Some have become quite liberal, allowing their members to use such modern conveniences as automobiles. Others remain very conservative, allowing no cars, no telephones, no central heating. These most conservative of the Amish are known as Old Order Amish.

God's Way

The Amish believe that their community, to be pleasing to God, must remain separate from the secular world. Their distinctive, uniform dress and radically simple way of life encourages both separation from the outside world and personal humility and simplicity. The Amish are pacifists and will not join the armed forces, even in time of war. Nor will the Amish work for the government or hold any public office that would entangle them in the affairs of the outside world. (They do, however, pay most taxes.) They will neither serve on juries nor defend their rights and interests in court.

The Amish also believe that, while human society is essentially sinful, nature—God's creation—is essentially good. They value work that keeps them close to nature, and value farming most of all. Farming is seen as stewardship of the land—maintaining God's gift of the earth so that it can be passed on to the next generation. Farming in the Amish manner involves the entire family, preferably a large family. It also involves the entire community, all of whom are expected to help one another in time of need, such as when someone falls sick or a barn has to be built. Old Order Amish will not participate in most forms of insurance, relying instead on God's providence and on their community.

Although Amish family farms produce most of what the family needs, the Amish are not subsistence farmers. A successful Amish farm will produce far more milk, eggs, meat, vegetables, or other farm products than the family needs. The surplus will be sold, some supplies will be bought with the proceeds, and whatever money is left over will be saved. The

Amish use their savings in time of need, but their primary purpose in saving money is to buy enough farmland to provide Amish family farms for their children.

Membership in an Amish community is voluntary and can be chosen only by adults. Teenagers who have been raised in the community who wish to remain in it when they become adults take a vow of baptism. Baptism seals a covenant between God and the individual taking the vow, who accepts spiritual salvation through Jesus Christ. In addition, however, the vow of baptism signifies full membership in and acceptance by the Amish community. Those who take the vow agree to observe all the customs of the community and to take on all the responsibilities required of a member of the community—for the rest of their lives.

If a member commits a sin and refuses to repent of it (anything from owning a car to committing adultery), or if a member causes or encourages other Amish to quarrel among themselves, or teaches a deviant religious doctrine, representatives of the community will warn the transgressor and try to persuade him or her to repent and be reconciled with the community. If the wayward member persists, he or she will be "shunned"—all members of the community will be forbidden to have anything to do with the person until he or she confesses the sin to the entire community in a Sunday church service and is forgiven and welcomed back. Shunning, if there is no reconciliation, can lead to being permanently cast out of the church—and the community. Parents may not speak to or share a meal with their shunned children; the husband or wife of a shunned member may not sleep with his or her spouse.

Shunning is a particularly painful punishment in such a close-knit community as the Amish. Most work is communal, and so are almost all forms of recreation—singing parties, barn-raisings, quilting parties, and above all, visiting. On Sundays (and on Saturdays, too, if work permits) most Amish families either go to visit their friends and relatives, or host visitors themselves. Shunned members who do not reconcile with their communities typically feel they must leave and make a home for themselves elsewhere.

Growing up Amish

Babies are always welcomed into Amish families as gifts of God. Although they are dressed simply and given few toys, babies are fed whenever they ask for it and are held and cuddled and fussed over a great deal by family and friends.

When a child begins to walk, its training and education also begin. Each child must learn right from wrong, and how to observe the customs of the community. Each child must also learn to respect others and to obey authority, mostly the authority of parents at first, but eventually also the authority of community leaders. And each child must learn to accept responsibility for doing useful work.

The nature of this work depends on whether the child is a boy or a girl. Amish men and women are mutually respectful partners whose roles are very distinct. Men do most of the heavy farmwork. Women tend to the house and garden (producing food for the family and for sale), and they bear many children—half a dozen or more is typical.

Although the entire community participates in minding its children, Amish parents are their children's most important teachers. Older children also watch over and instruct their younger siblings, and so do grandparents, who usually live with their adult children, offering and receiving assistance. Fathers are considered essential for their sons' education. There is no provision for divorce among the Amish, and single parenting is simply not done.

Mostly, parents teach by example. Mothers will bring their daughters and young sons along as they go about working in the house and around the farm, showing them how the work is done and assigning them tasks that are appropriate for the children's ages. Sons go with their fathers into the fields, where they learn how to farm by doing it.

For such a pervasively religious community, there is surprisingly little formal prayer outside of church—usually silent prayer before and after meals, and at bedtime. Although children are not considered church members, they attend church with their parents. Church services are not held in a church, but circulate among members' homes, which are built with this need in mind. (Doors open wide or walls fold back, joining rooms together to fit in enough wooden benches to seat as many as 200 or more, and then to serve everyone a meal after the hours-long service.) The usual Christian holidays are celebrated—each child typically receives a toy on Christmas—but the two biggest holidays of the year are the spring and fall communion services, when everyone in the community renews the commitment to the Amish religion and to each other.

When children reach school age, they usually attend a small, local, Amish-controlled school and continue to work with the family during off-school

Amish children learn the ways of farm life by doing. Here a young child accompanies her mother on a farm chore.

hours. (Early in the twentieth century, many rural one-room public schools were closed and their students assigned to larger school districts. Many Amish parents resisted sending their children so far away to schools not so tightly controlled by the Amish. Some parents went to jail rather than do so.) Amish "scholars," as they are called, on average do as well as their non-Amish peers in basic reading, writing, and arithmetic. In addition to the usual academic skills, Amish schools are expected to reinforce the parents' and the community's efforts to teach children discipline and how to get along with others.

Formal schooling for Amish children ends with the eighth grade. After that, they receive vocational training by working with their families. Some youths work with other Amish families, or even for non-Amish employers. During their teenage years, children are expected to work hard, but their parents allow them a great deal of freedom and privacy. The Amish believe that in order to choose freely whether or not to join the community as adults, young men and women must know something of the outside world. So, during this adolescent period of exploration, a young man may, for example, semisecretly acquire a driver's license or even a car, while his parents look the other way.

Amish young adults deciding whether to join the church are also coming to grips with the other great decision of their lives: whom to marry. Nearly all Amish marry, and no Amish person may marry a non-Amish person. (Marriage between members of different communities that are in full fellowship is permitted.) Amish youths who choose to remain Amish usually are baptized and become church members at about twenty years of age and are married in their mid-twenties. Weddings are usually held in the late fall or early winter, after the harvest is finished, and they are community-wide celebrations.

"When Do We Leave?"

Some young adults decide not to become Amish and leave the community. Although they may stay in touch with their families, they will not be able to share in the intimate closeness that the Amish cultivate among themselves.

Through the years, most young people have decided to stay. In the past century, in fact, the Amish have had so many children, and so many of them have decided to remain Amish, that the population of their communities has grown from an estimated 3,700 in 1890 to 128,000 in 1990. In the past twenty years alone, their population has doubled—and this despite the fact that the Amish do not seek converts from outside their communities.[2]

When young people do decide to leave, more and more often their decision is related to difficulty with finding enough farmland to support them. In the long-established Amish communities near Lancaster, these difficulties have become particularly urgent. For many Old Order Amish, the question has become not whether to leave, but "*When* do we leave?"

For several generations, as the Amish population has grown rapidly, many parents in the area have found it difficult to find enough affordable farmland for their children. For many years, land was purchased from non-Amish neighbors leaving the land

It can be startling to see the world of the Amish in contrast with the world of outsiders. Amish buggies share roads with cars and trucks, and Amish people utilize some modern conveniences, such as grocery stores.

for work in cities. But now Amish country has become crowded. Farms have been subdivided into such small units that each can barely support a family. Many Amish have been forced into nonfarming work—mostly reluctantly, for children of nonfarming Amish are much less likely to grow up and choose to become Amish themselves.

Some have earned money through tourism. The "Pennsylvania Dutch," as outsiders have called them, have long been a major tourist attraction. Hundreds of tourism-related enterprises—restaurants and motels, gift shops and outlet malls—cater to tourists interested in visiting Amish country. For every Amish person living near Lancaster, several hundred tourists pass through each year, pumping millions of dollars into the local economy.

By and large, the Amish have neither encouraged nor discouraged tourism, which they consider foolishness. It is of the "outside" world and hence no concern of theirs. Most Amish simply go about their business, attempting to ignore the tourists who clog their narrow rural roads, eager to snap their pictures. But many Amish—mostly those who don't have the land to be full-time farmers—have themselves profited from tourism, most commonly by selling produce or handcrafts.

Tourism means crowds, and that means still more pressure on a community already too crowded on its land. A far greater threat than the tourism, however, has turned out to be development. Philadelphia's suburban sprawl has spread toward Lancaster. Factories and other business enterprises have sprung up where once there was only farmland, and their workers need housing. "More people from our larger cities want to live in our section of the country," one Amish historian has written. "For that reason more homes need to be built. . . . Every year, thousands of acres of highly productive farmland is being used in building developments, new roads and factories, making the price of farmland more competitive to the extent that the Amish people are being pressed to move to other areas where they can enjoy a more peaceful form of life."[3]

Setting their children up with their own nearby family farms—either by giving them the land or by helping them to buy it—has for hundreds of years been the central life goal of generations of Amish parents. Now, for more and more of the Lancaster-area Amish, this goal is out of reach. No matter how hard they work and how carefully they save, small-scale farmers can't afford to pay development-inflated prices for land. If their children are to remain Amish, they'll have to move to other parts of the country, where land is cheaper. And the community will break apart.

"Two hundred years ago, or more, our people came here to escape religious persecution in Europe, and in those days the countryside was mostly woods," one Amish man from Lancaster reflected at a 1990 hearing on a new housing development. "Well, we helped to turn the land into what is now called the garden spot of the world, but if this development keeps up it looks as if we're going to be driven out again. This time it will not be religious persecution, it will be the persecution of prosperity."[4]

SHAKERS

"THE PECULIAR GRACE OF A SHAKER CHAIR IS DUE
TO THE FACT THAT IT WAS MADE BY SOMEONE CA-
PABLE OF BELIEVING THAT AN ANGEL MIGHT COME
AND SIT ON IT."

—THOMAS MERTON [1]

Like the Amish, the Shakers came to America in colonial times to escape religious persecution in Europe.
Unlike the Amish, their numbers have dwindled to
near disappearance. Their influence, however, is as
strong as it has ever been—inspiring countless
American craftsmen and artists.

A Sect on the Rise

Shakerism grew out of the faith of a small band of
eighteenth-century English believers inspired by the
religious vision of Ann Lee, an illiterate woman
whose penniless family had married her off, against
her will, to a blacksmith, whom she eventually abandoned. Like the Anabaptists, Lee and her fellow
Shakers were radical Protestants. Their raucous

Shaker-made items are known for their simplicity, function, and ingenuity of design.

church services—where they shook with religious fervor, sang loudly, and danced ecstatically—scandalized their more conventional neighbors. They were violently persecuted in England. Unlike the Anabaptists, however, they were fewer than a dozen in number when they left England for America in 1774.

Little is known about the Shakers during those early years. When they arrived in New York, they apparently scattered and lived separately for a time before establishing a small community—called Niskeyuna—in what was then western wilderness, near Albany, New York. There they felled trees, created farms, and built homes for themselves, while continuing to practice their religion and preach it to whomever sought them out. "Put your hands to work and your hearts to God," Ann Lee is said to have told her followers.[2]

As pacifists, the Shakers refused to participate in the Revolutionary War, and several of them—including Ann Lee—went to jail as a result. After they were released from prison, in 1781, Ann Lee and the sect's other two leaders, Ann's brother William Lee and James Whittaker, embarked on more than two years of missionary travels throughout New England.

While the Shaker missionaries made many converts, they also encountered much hostility to their unusual version of Christianity, which, for example, emphasized that God was feminine and nurturing as well as masculine and fierce:

As *Father*, God is the infinite Fountain of intelligence, and the source of all power—"the Almighty, great and terrible in majesty"; "the high and lofty one, that inhabiteth eternity, whose name is Holy, dwelling in the high and holy place"; and "a consuming fire." But as *Mother*, *"God is Love"* and tenderness. If all the maternal affections of all female or bearing spirits in animated nature were combined together, and then concentrated in *one individual female*, that person would be but as a type or image of our Eternal Heavenly Mother.[3]

Shakers came to believe that the "Eternal Heavenly Mother" in the flesh, come to Earth, was their leader Ann Lee.

Travel in the late 1700s was arduous, and being on the road for so long took a terrible physical toll on the three missionaries. They returned home toward the end of 1783. William Lee died the following July, and his sister Ann followed him two months later. Leadership among the Shakers had always been shared by several believers—not entirely embodied in Ann Lee—and this may have made it easier for the sect to survive the death of its preeminent founder. Saddened, but not defeated, the Shaker community lived on.

James Whittaker, who took over leadership of the sect, was not only a stirring preacher but also an able administrator and manager. He encouraged the "gathering" of the Shakers scattered around New England into self-sufficient communities, set apart from the world, living a Shaker life by Shaker rules. Before much of this gathering could be accomplished, however, Whittaker died, in 1787.

After Whittaker's death, Joseph Meacham soon emerged as the Shakers' new primary leader. Meacham, a Baptist leader converted to Shakerism

The religious services of the United Society of Believers in Christ's Second Appearing included dancing and ecstatic movements, and looked odd to outsiders. It was the very nature of these services that led the sect to be called the Shakers.

by Ann Lee herself, had led much of his former flock in New Lebanon, New York, into the Shaker fold. Meacham made New Lebanon the center of Shakerism. He continued the "gathering" work begun by Whittaker. He also started the sect on the path of writing down what Shakers believed, and the rules by which they worshipped and lived. And, in keeping with the Shakers' belief in God's feminine aspect and in the appropriateness of women as spiritual leaders, Meacham shared his leadership role with a woman, Lucy Wright. She took over primary leadership of the Shakers after Meacham's death, in 1796.

Wright led the Shakers through a quarter of a century of strong growth. Her greatest talent, perhaps, was for sustaining unity among the Shakers' far-flung communities while encouraging new converts and the establishment of new communities. By the time Wright died, in 1827, several thousand Shakers lived in no fewer than nineteen separate communities. Most of the Shaker communities were clustered in New England, from southern Maine to eastern and central New York. However, as a result of the tireless work of David Darrow, the Shakers' other great leader during these years of growth, seven new communities were founded in the Midwest—dotted across Ohio, Indiana, and Kentucky.

The early 1800s were the glory years for Shakerism as a way of life. Never again would there be so many Shaker communities, nor so many Shakers.

Shaker Beliefs and Lifestyle

Shaker beliefs developed and changed over the years. The earliest Shakers—Ann Lee and her colleagues—never wrote down any of their preaching. Later Shakers built on and adapted the remembered ideas of the founders to meet the needs of the growing sect in changing times.

Some Shaker beliefs remained constant. One belief was that sex was a formerly necessary evil that, in the new Shaker age, had outlived its usefulness. Shaker men and women were celibate—they lived and worked together as brothers and sisters, but not as husbands and wives. If a married couple joined the Shakers (and quite a few did), they gave up sex and agreed to treat one another as no more or less than another Shaker brother or sister. If they brought children into the community with them, they were raised by the community as a whole and not just by their birth parents.

The Shakers also rejected the idea of private property. They lived communally: Converts gave up all of their possessions when they joined the Shakers, and in turn they shared in the use of all of their community's collective resources. Shaker communities, however, were not democracies. Each individual was expected to submit obediently to his or her appointed leaders. Leaders, though, were expected to govern in a spirit of loving unity, and all community members were to be valued and loved as bearers of God's gifts. The *United* Society of Believers was the Shakers' formal name, and unity was very important to them.

All of the adult members of a Shaker "family"— as many as dozens of men and women—typically slept dormitory-style, with women occupying one side and men the other of one large building. Some Shaker communities included a half dozen families; two or three was more usual. A Shaker spent little time alone, sharing a sleeping room with several other men or women,

The Shaker village in Hancock, Massachusetts, was a thriving, fully functioning community for much of the nineteenth century. The round stone barn at the right side of the picture is a distinctive landmark there.

rising at dawn with the rest of the family, eating and praying with the entire family, and working together with other men or women at appointed tasks.

Men and women did different kinds of work, divided along fairly traditional lines. Men handled the heavier farmwork and carpentry, for example, while women cooked and sewed. However, both sexes played leadership roles (elders and eldresses, deacons and deaconesses), and women were considered to be as spiritually gifted as men.

Both men and women produced "fancy goods" for sale to the world outside their community—from vegetable and herb seeds to cloaks, boxes, baskets, and furniture. Although the Shakers rejected private property, they did not object to commerce. Different communities specialized in different goods, which became well known and valued for their exceptional quality.

Unlike the Amish, the Shakers were not religiously suspicious of technology. On the contrary, they were fabulously inventive and created elegant devices to simplify and ease their work. Many of these devices—most famously the flat broom, the clothespin, and the circular saw—have made their way into common use.

The Shakers had a religious mandate for the quality of their work. Shaker religion wasn't merely— or even primarily—something practiced in religious services. It was a way of life, with Shaker spirituality permeating every thought and action. "Do all your work as though you had a thousand years to live, and as you would if you knew you must die tomorrow," is how Ann Lee reportedly put it.[4] The Shakers believed that the second coming of Christ—the feminine manifestation, in the person of Ann Lee—had enabled believers to live in perfection, without sin. This perfection was to be shown in love not only for fellow Shakers but also for outsiders. (Shakers continued to refuse to participate in any war, and they would feed anyone who showed up at their door hungry.) And it was to be shown in Shakers' orderly and peaceful lives, in their clean and uncluttered rooms, and in their work, which was to be done beautifully, perfectly, but simply, without distraction, with purity of purpose.

"We are not called upon to labor to excel, or to be like the world," one Shaker elder said, "but to excel them in order, union, peace and in good works—works that are truly virtuous and useful to man in this life. . . . All work done or things made [by Shakers] . . . ought to be faithfully and well done but plain and without superfluity. All things ought to be made according to their order and use."[5]

Vanishing Communities

Beginning in 1837, Shaker communities from Maine to Kentucky experienced a wave of spiritual turbulence and revival that came to be known as the "Era of Manifestations" or "Mother Ann's Work," after Ann Lee. Lee's spirit was credited as the chief moving force behind all manner of extraordinary actions by believers—from frenzied dancing to singing unknown songs to speaking in spirit voices to seeing visions. Eventually, in the late 1840s, the spiritual storm of Mother Ann's Work dissipated, although many Shakers remained keenly interested in contact with the spirit world. The most tangible legacies of

Mother Ann's Work were hundreds of new hymns inspired by spiritual experiences, and "spirit drawings" made to copy down what the artists saw in dreams or visions. The best known of these spirit drawings are the Tree of Life drawings from the Shaker village near Hancock, Massachusetts.

Even as Mother Ann's Work was under way, though, Shaker communities were losing a worrisome number of members. Many who left were children who had entered Shaker communities with their parents, or as orphans, or as indentured servants or apprentices, and who chose not to remain after they grew up. (So common was it to send children to the Shakers that nearly one fifth of those living at the celibate Shaker villages in 1820 were under the age of sixteen.)[6] Many others, however, were adults who had willingly joined the communities but later had become disenchanted with Shaker life.

By 1860, markedly more members were slipping away from Shaker communities than were joining them, and the rate of loss was accelerating. (Obviously, the celibate Shakers didn't increase their number through childbirth.) The number of Shakers on the membership list slipped from 3,627 in 1840, to 3,489 in 1860, to 1,849 in 1880, and only 855 at the turn of the century.[7]

At the same time as the number of Shakers was shrinking, their distinctiveness and separateness from the world was fading. Shaker dress, which never was entirely uniform, became still more flexible and more like what was in fashion in the outside world. Shaker religious services became more like those in mainstream Protestant churches. Even clean-lined Shaker architecture bent to fashion in some communities: At Hancock, for example, the pure and austere trustees' house and office received a high-Victorian makeover in 1895.

Faced with the dwindling numbers of Shakers— too few of them to keep up the businesses and buildings at all the scattered Shaker communities—the central Shaker ministry began to close down some of its communities, selling off their assets and relocating the remaining Shakers. Many of the typically elderly and female Shakers forced to leave the homes that they had loved for decades found the move painfully difficult. "The sisters are very kind," one Shaker wrote about her new home, "but this dark house is very depressing to an already broken heart. [T]he hills smother me and this room crushes me. Home is where the heart is and mine is not here."[8]

By 1925, only six Shaker villages remained: the original settlement near Albany (by this time known as Watervliet) and the settlements at New Lebanon; Hancock; Canterbury, New Hampshire; Alfred, Maine; and Sabbathday Lake, Maine. By the mid-1990s, only Sabbathday Lake remained as an active Shaker community, with only a half dozen living as Shakers there.

Esthetic Legacy

Even as the Shaker communities were dying, interest in their artifacts—their chairs and tables, buildings and baskets—took root and flourished in mainstream America. Seen through the objects they created, Shakers became known as skilled and painstaking craftsmen with a unique esthetic sensibility reflecting their unique religious beliefs.

More than any single individual, an antiques dealer and writer named Edward Deming Andrews was responsible for making Shaker style so popular. Over several decades, but especially with his popular 1953 history *The People Called Shakers*, Andrews created and polished what has become the prevailing image of Shaker esthetics. Among the Shakers, Andrews wrote:

> The practical arts were not deprecated as inferior to the fine. Beauty was inherent in a product fashioned to meet the needs of a life based on contemplation and dedicated to rectitude.
>
> Builders and joiners, therefore, inevitably impressed their character, the Shaker character, upon their work. . . . Reflecting the preference for plainness and subdued, uniform colors, the furnishings of Shaker rooms naturally harmonized with their white plastered walls, the reddish-yellow floors, oiled and neatly carpeted, the doors, window frames, and delicately turned wall pegs of mellow brown. No distracting elements violated the quiet simplicity of these airy, well-lighted interiors. The colors glowed softly. . . . A spirit of peace, almost of sanctity, pervaded the scene.[9]

Others soon followed in Andrews's footsteps—a torrent of filmmakers, scholarly researchers, and newspaper and magazine reporters overwhelmed the few remaining Shakers with requests for information. Furniture dealers, art collectors, and museums came as well. Since the 1950s, the market for authentic Shaker antiques has soared, with some exceptionally fine pieces fetching hundreds of thousands of dollars at auction. Even *reproductions* of Shaker furniture command premium prices.

In a few places, Shaker enthusiasts have purchased whole sets of buildings abandoned by the Shakers, restored and refurbished them, and opened them to the public as museums. At other former Shaker villages, buildings and land have been put to various uses. In most of these places, faint traces are all that is left of the Shakers today.

MORMONS

"I TELL YOU MORMONISM IS ONE GREAT SURGE OF
LICENTIOUSNESS; IT IS THE SERAGLIO OF THE RE-
PUBLIC, IT IS THE CONCENTRATED CORRUPTION OF
THIS LAND, IT IS THE BROTHEL OF THE NATION, IT
IS HELL ENTHRONED. THIS MISERABLE CORPSE OF
MORMONISM HAS BEEN ROTTING IN THE SUN, AND
ROTTING AND ROTTING FOR FORTY YEARS, AND THE
UNITED STATES GOVERNMENT HAS NOT HAD THE
COURAGE TO BURY IT."
                    — A PROTESTANT PREACHER IN 1880[1]

In only a century and a half, the Church of Jesus
Christ of Latter-day Saints has grown from a tiny,
viciously persecuted sect into today's powerful,
wealthy, multimillion-member church. Even today,
however, it is in conflict with America's mainstream
values and lifestyles, especially concerning its beliefs
and restrictions on the roles of women.

The Prophet Joseph Smith

About 1820, Joseph Smith, a teenage boy living in
western New York, began having visions. First, he

The Church of Jesus Christ of Latter-Day Saints, also known as the Mormons, is one religious movement that began outside the mainstream and that not only survived, but has grown to be a major part of American religious life.

saw God the Father and his son Jesus in a pillar of light, speaking directly to him. On a September night in 1823, he had a second vision:

> A light appeared in the room which continued to increase until the room was lighter than at noonday, when immediately a personage appeared at my bedside, standing in the air, for his feet did not touch the floor. . . . He called me by name, and said unto me that he was a messenger sent from the presence of God to me, and that his name was Moroni. That God had work for me to do. . . . He said that there was a book deposited written upon gold plates, giving an account of the former inhabitants of this continent, and the source from whence they sprang.[2]

According to Joseph Smith, the angel Moroni told him where to find these gold plates, and over several years he translated and wrote down what he found written on them. The results of Smith's experiences were the *Book of Mormon*, and a new religion.

The *Book of Mormon* tells the story of a small band of Hebrews, God's chosen people, who came to America from Jerusalem before the time of Christ. In America, they divided into two warring groups, and built great cities and temples. Jesus appeared to these people after his resurrection, inspiring two centuries of peace and harmony. Eventually, however, the people split once again into warring factions, and after much death and destruction blended with immigrants from Europe and Asia to become the Native Americans known to Columbus and later generations of European colonists. Their story, written down by their last prophet, Moroni, remained hidden until Joseph Smith was told in his vision where to find it.

Smith and his small band of followers formally organized their new church, the Church of Jesus Christ of Latter-day Saints, in 1830. They called themselves "Saints" and believed that their church was the true heir of the original Christian church, which they believed had long gone astray from God's plan.

What do Mormons believe? First and foremost, that God has once again begun speaking directly to humankind, as in the days described in Jewish and Christian scripture. Part of God's new message is in the *Book of Mormon*, a supplement to (not a substitute for) the Old and New Testaments; in addition, God reveals other truths from time to time directly to prophets (such as Smith) whom God deems worthy. Second, that with the guidance of this prophecy God's church—constituted as the Church of Jesus Christ of Latter-day Saints—has been restored to its proper form and function. Third, that through this church spiritual gifts not seen since the earliest days of Christianity are once again available to those who wholeheartedly join and obey the church.

Non-Mormons from the very beginning found these ideas heretical and offensive. They also felt threatened by the Mormons' solidarity—the way the church acted in a unified, coordinated way in economic and political as well as church-related matters. They persecuted the Mormons relentlessly.

Dodging persecution ranging from vandalism to lynching, the small but ever-increasing band of Mormons migrated several times in the early years of the church. For a time they settled in Missouri. "The Mormons must be treated as enemies," that state's Governor Lilburn W. Boggs said in 1838, "and must be exterminated or driven from the State if necessary, for the public peace."[3]

The following year, Smith led his followers to an uninhabited corner of Illinois, on the Mississippi River, where they built the city of Nauvoo. There, because of the Mormons' strong and wide-ranging missionary activity, their numbers increased rapidly.

Sadly, Nauvoo proved to be no safe haven. Hostility to and violence against Mormons continued. In 1844, Joseph Smith and several of his colleagues were arrested and taken to jail some miles distant from Nauvoo. There, a lynch mob overran the jail and murdered Smith.

Gathering at the Great Basin

Soon after Smith's death, earnest and energetic Brigham Young emerged as the Mormons' new leader. In 1846 he led the Mormons out of Nauvoo toward a new home in the West.

The Great Basin, in what is now Utah, where the Mormons settled in 1847 to build their church-centered community, was a harsh environment. Hemmed in by mountains to the east and west, stretching south to the Colorado River and north to the Columbia River's watershed, the Great Basin had weather that was too dry for many crops, and its winters were hard. But the region's very inhospitableness and isolation were part of its appeal to Brigham Young and the other Mormon leaders. Here, in a land no one else wanted, the Mormons might finally be left in peace.

Soon, though, conflict with non-Mormons began anew. After a couple of difficult winters, the new Mormon community, concentrated in the valley of the Great Salt Lake, grew by the thousands and thrived. Converts from back East, and even tens of thousands of converts from Europe, migrated to Mormon country in the latter half of the 1800s.

But so, increasingly, did non-Mormons. As the United States' Western frontier filled up with migrants seeking their fortune, the Mormons' homeland became less and less isolated. Non-Mormons increasingly complained about the Mormons' strange ways. The strangest of these ways, to outsiders, and the one condemned most loudly by non-Mormons, was the practice of polygamy: Mormon men taking more than one wife.

Since as early as the 1840s, Mormon leaders—Joseph Smith among them—had reasoned that "plurality of wives is taught in the Bible, that Abraham, Jacob, Solomon, David and indeed all the old prophets and good men had several wives, and if it is all right for them, it is all right for the Latter Day Saints."[4]

"Early in the year 1842," one Mormon woman later recalled, "Joseph Smith taught me the principle of marriage for eternity, and the doctrine of plural marriage. He said that in teaching this he realized that he jeopardized his life; but God had revealed it to him many years before as a privilege with blessings, now God had revealed it again and instructed him to teach it with commandment. . . . I asked him to teach it to some one else."[5] Nor did Smith's own wife, Emma Smith, approve. She voiced her opposition to polygamy, even while her husband apparently practiced it.

Brigham Young's faith and pioneering spirit brought the Mormons to Utah in 1847 but more religious persecution awaited the group.

Although many, or perhaps most, of them practiced polygamy themselves, Mormon leaders kept quiet about the matter until 1852, when they were well established in the remote Salt Lake Valley. There and then they began openly to encourage their followers to enter "plural marriages."

Mormon polygamy not only outraged mainstream morality but also ran against U.S. law. Public pressure to end polygamy increased as knowledge of the practice spread outside the Mormon community. Many Mormon leaders were jailed for polygamy in the 1880s.

The issue of polygamy became the central roadblock to Mormon-dominated Utah becoming a state, and to Mormons gaining all the rights and privileges of U.S. citizens. Although today Americans see the shaping of the state of Utah as the Mormons' most obvious contribution to American life, a century ago opposition to Mormonism nearly prevented Utah's statehood from being granted.

On September 25, 1890, Mormon President Wilford Woodruff issued the statement known among Mormons as the Manifesto: "Inasmuch as laws have been enacted by Congress forbidding plural marriages, which laws have been pronounced constitutional by the court of last resort [the Supreme Court], I hereby declare my intention to submit to those laws, and to use my influence with the members of the Church over which I preside to have them do likewise."[6] The way was cleared for Utah to become a state. Since the Manifesto, only a few Mormon fundamentalists have persisted in forming plural marriages, and the church leadership has consistently refused to approve them.

Change and Growth

The Mormon church made several changes around the turn of the century to resolve its conflicts with mainstream America.

The first and most obvious of these changes was the abandonment of polygamy. Other changes were quieter, but nonetheless deeply important. Once Utah achieved statehood, for example, Mormons were encouraged to join the Republican or Democratic party (rather than maintain a separate political organization, as they had done in the past) and thereby join the political mainstream.

Nearly as much at odds with the American mainstream as polygamy was the early Mormon community's near-communal economic solidarity. "We do not intend to have any trade or commerce with the Gentile [non-Mormon] world," Brigham Young had said soon after the Saints' arrival in the Salt Lake Valley, "for so long as we buy of them we are in a degree dependent upon them. The Kingdom of God cannot rise independent of the Gentile nations until we produce, manufacture, and make every article of use, convenience, or necessity among our own people."[7]

Early in this century, however, the Mormons shifted to mainstream American capitalism. Individual Mormons were encouraged to compete and do well in business, playing by the same rules as everybody else. Although the church continued to operate some businesses, its members were expected to earn their livelihood without special assistance from the church. This pattern still holds true today.

As the Mormons changed their ways to fit in with their neighbors, persecution of Mormons in

America ceased, allowing the Mormons to achieve extraordinary growth and prosperity. Today, as a result of several generations of large Mormon families and decades of extensive missionary work (all young Mormon men are strongly encouraged to serve a two-year turn as missionaries), there are some 4.5 million Mormons worldwide.

In recent years, church authorities have made another change that better aligns the church with mainstream America by granting full equality to black Mormons. For many years, although Mormon missionaries sought black converts, the church held that "Negroes [are] not yet to receive the priesthood, for reasons which we believe are known to God, but which He has not made fully known to man."[8] In 1978 the church's top leaders announced that, in their role as prophets, God had revealed to them that "all worthy male members of the Church may be ordained to the priesthood without regard for race or color."[9]

Women's Proper Place

The change in the status of blacks in the Mormon church came in the context of the many changes in the status of blacks in American society brought about by the civil-rights movement of the 1960s. Similar changes have occurred in recent years in the status of women in the United States. But no such change has occurred in the status of Mormon women within their church.

The place of women in Mormon society has been subservient but not without strength. On the one hand, although all "worthy" men (those who live by church rules) are eligible and encouraged to be priests, the priesthood is for men only, and the entire church leadership is therefore made up of men, most of them middle-aged or elderly. Furthermore, Mormon men are supposed to be the heads of their families, and wives are expected to submit to their husbands' authority. Motherhood and wifely duty are considered a Mormon woman's highest callings. This, the Mormons believe, is the eternal order of things—it will hold in Heaven as well as on Earth.

On the other hand, Mormon men cannot fulfill their highest spiritual calling unless they grow together with their wives through marriage—they can't go it alone. In addition, strong and resourceful women have been needed since the earliest days of the faith to build the Mormons' new home in the West and to run homes and family businesses while their husbands are away for long stretches on church business. Brigham Young himself once said: "We believe that women are useful, not only to sweep houses, wash dishes, make beds, and raise babies, but that they should stand behind the counter, study law or physic [medicine], or become good book-keepers and be able to do the business in any counting house, and all this to enlarge their sphere of usefulness for the benefit of society at large. In following these things they but answer the design of their creation."[10]

The year Young made this statement, in 1869, nearly the same number of Mormon women as men were attending college at the University of Deseret, at a time when few non-Mormon women attended college anywhere else. At the same time, Mormon women could and did vote in Utah. Some even held public office, until the U.S. Congress took away their voting rights in 1887. (They got the vote back with the rest of America's women, in 1921.) In addition, various church organizations since the days of Joseph Smith have encouraged and facilitated Mormon women's accomplishments outside the home, from fund-raising to cooperative businesses.

As Mormon culture became more mainstream American, however, the expectations for women began to change. In the 1960s and 1970s especially, the church transferred much of the control over Mormon women's organizations to men and increasingly emphasized women's at-home role. The church authorities had taken notice of the growing American women's movement, and they didn't like it. By 1980, their message to Mormon women was clear: "Homemaking is the highest, most noble profession to which a woman might aspire," the prominent Mormon leader Ezra Taft Benson told one group of women. "Support, encourage, and strengthen your husband in his responsibility as patriarch in the home. A woman's role in a man's life is to lift him, to help him uphold lofty standards, and to prepare through righteous living to be his queen for all eternity."[11]

While most Mormon women accepted these ideas, some questioned them. How well did these ideals of womanhood really fit with modern reality, with more and more Mormon women—like other American women—both working outside their homes and more economically vulnerable to divorce than they had been in the past? Were these ideals really what God intended? A group of Mormon women in Boston in the 1970s were particularly active and vocal in trying to reconcile their faith with feminism. One of them explained:

The standard for Mormon womanhood is the supportive wife, the loving mother of many, the excellent cook, the imaginative homemaker and the diligent Church worker, a woman whose life is circumscribed by these roles. This model has been so clearly presented to us in sermon and story that we feel strong responsibility to cleave to that ideal and guilt when we depart. And so our group, largely made up of supportive wives and loving mothers who are also excellent homemakers and Church workers, has discussed the genesis of that model, how much of it is scriptural and how much traditional, and whether other models have met with acceptance in Church history.[12]

Push came to shove for Mormon feminists in the late 1970s over the Equal Rights Amendment (ERA), a proposed constitutional amendment intended to give women legal equality with men. The Mormon church mounted a successful campaign to prevent the ERA's ratification in several key states. Some Mormon women objected.

Foremost among these was Sonia Johnson, a lifelong Mormon, a mother of four children, and an appealing public speaker. Johnson spoke out in favor of the ERA. Church authorities told her to stop, and she refused.

Johnson saw her church's opposition to the ERA as part of a broader pattern of oppressing women. For too long, she believed, Mormon women had ac-

Sonia Johnson was excommunicated from the Mormon church for her vocal support of the Equal Rights Amendment for women. The amendment seemed to challenge directly many of the church's teachings in regard to women and their role.

quiesced—out of fear. "Where the Mormons and other fundamentalist religionists keep patriarchy sacred on their altars," she later wrote, "women *do* fear that . . . if they are not subservient, men won't love them. If men don't love them, God won't love them. Everything will go wrong in their lives if they lose the support of men, which means losing the support of God and of their society."[13]

Ultimately, a Mormon bishop's court told Sonia Johnson: "The decision of this court is that you are excommunicated from the Church of Jesus Christ of Latter-day Saints. . . . I strongly encourage you to repent."

"Repent of what, I wonder now," she wrote several months later. "Of being happier than I have ever been in my life?"[14]

CATHOLIC WORKERS

"YES, THE POOR ARE ALWAYS GOING TO BE WITH US—OUR LORD TOLD US THAT—AND THERE WILL ALWAYS BE A NEED FOR OUR SHARING, FOR STRIP-PING OURSELVES TO HELP OTHERS.IT WILL ALWAYS BE A LIFETIME JOB.

BUT I AM SURE THAT GOD DID NOT INTEND THAT THERE BE SO MANY POOR. THE CLASS STRUCTURE IS OF OUR MAKING AND BY OUR CONSENT, NOT HIS, AND WE MUST DO WHAT WE CAN TO CHANGE IT .SO WE ARE URGING REVOLUTIONARY CHANGE."
— DOROTHY DAY[1]

Catholicism and socialism were enemies in the United States—until the Catholic Worker movement joined them in compassionate service to the poor.

Dorothy Day

Dorothy Day, born in 1897, grew up into a restless youth. She dropped out of college and migrated from Illinois to New York City's bohemian Greenwich Vil-

A group of Catholic Workers gather outside the organization's New York headquarters in the early 1930s. The Workers combined Catholicism and Socialism in a movement to help the poor and promote peace.

lage, where she lived and worked among artists and writers and political radicals in the late teens and early 1920s. A writer and a socialist, she reported on subjects ranging from strikes and picket lines to birth control and tenement evictions. She went to jail for picketing at the White House. She fell in love, became pregnant, and had an abortion, and then her lover left her. She traveled, wrote, and set up housekeeping with another man.

In 1926, Day gave birth to a daughter. By this time, she was finding herself more and more drawn to the mystical, spiritual meaning—although not the conservative social practices—of the Catholic Church. "I loved the Church for Christ made visible," she later recalled. "Not for itself, because it was so often a scandal to me."[2]

Day had her baby daughter baptized in the faith. The father of the child, an atheist, was repulsed by Day's growing religiousness. According to Day, "it got to the point where it was the simple question of whether I chose God or man."[3] Day chose God, and became a Catholic. She began attending Mass daily, a practice that she kept up for the rest of her life.

Peter Maurin

For several years, Day longed to find a way to reconcile and integrate her radical politics with her newfound Catholic spirituality. The Communists she knew were atheists who looked on religion as "the opiate of the masses," a drug that sapped workers' will for revolution. Catholics, on the other had, saw communism as an unchangeable enemy of the church. Then, in 1932, Day met Peter Maurin, who showed her the way.

Peter Maurin was a learned and passionate saint in the humblest of earthly appearances—a "holy fool." A child of a huge and penniless family of French peasants (he had twenty-two brothers and sisters), Maurin had come to North America in 1909, when he was in his early thirties. He practiced voluntary poverty, exchanging his labor for food and shelter, giving away whatever he acquired, often sleeping in his only set of clothes in a cheap hotel. He read voraciously, and over time he developed a comprehensive, radical, Catholic social philosophy, a strategy for mending what he saw as the root of all evil in the modern world: the separation between God and human economic, social, and political life.

"I certainly didn't realize at first that I had my answer in Peter Maurin," Day wrote years later. "I was thirty-five years old and I had met plenty of radicals in my time, and plenty of crackpots, too."[4]

Nonetheless, Day soon decided that Maurin was *not* a crackpot, and that his life's mission should be hers as well. "Peter made you feel a sense of his mission as soon as you met him," she later wrote. "He did not begin by tearing down, or by painting so intense a picture of misery and injustice that you burned to change the world. Instead, he aroused in you a sense of your own capacities for work, for accomplishment. He made you feel that you and all men had great and generous hearts with which to love God. If you once recognized this fact in yourself you would expect to find it in others."[5]

Three-Point Program

"We need to make the kind of society . . . where it is easier for people to be good," Maurin often said, and he ceaselessly promoted a three-point program for doing so.[6] These three points became the heart and soul of the Catholic Worker movement:

- *Point One:* "clarification of thought." In meetings for discussion, and through lectures and publications, people would discuss and come to adopt as their own radical Catholic ideas for social revolution.

- *Point Two:* "Houses of Hospitality." In every city—in every parish, even—Catholics committed to caring for their neighbors as they would for Christ himself would provide food and shelter for the needy.

- *Point Three*: "agronomic universities." On communal farms, a radically new, noncapitalist, non-Communist way of life would be created—cooperative and respectful of workers' humanity, rather than acquisitive and exploitative.

"As Peter pointed out," Day wrote, "ours was a long-range program, looking for ownership by the workers of the means of production, the abolition of the assembly line, decentralized factories, the restoration of crafts and ownership of property."[7] This was radical Catholicism indeed. Nothing like it had ever been seen in America.

Catholic Workers in Action

As their first step in this program, Day and Maurin started a newspaper offering sympathetic reporting on workers' issues and a radical, Catholic perspective on the events of the day. They called their newspaper *The Catholic Worker* and sold it at a price anyone could afford: a penny a copy. Edited by Day, a talented and experienced journalist, *The Catholic Worker*'s high standards of quality, distinctive voice, and passionately appealing content made the paper a long-running success.

"*The Catholic Worker*, as the name implied," Day later wrote, "was directed to the worker, but we used the word in its broadest sense, meaning those who worked with hand or brain, those who did physical, mental, or spiritual work. But we thought primarily of the poor, the dispossessed, the exploited. . . . We felt a respect for the poor and destitute as those nearest to God, as those chosen by Christ for His compassion."[8] Day believed that

> Christ is always with us, always asking for room in our hearts. But now it is with the voices of our contemporaries that He speaks, with the eyes of store clerks, factory workers, and children that He gazes; with the hands of office workers, slum dwellers, and suburban housewives that He gives. It is with the feet of soldiers and tramps that He walks, and with the heart of anyone in need that He longs for shelter. And giving shelter or food to anyone who asks for it, or needs it, is giving it to Christ.[9]

To this end, Day and Maurin and their colleagues began to feed the hungry and shelter the homeless at the building where they published the paper and where they and other Catholic Workers lived communally—the first House of Hospitality. No one drew

The *Catholic Worker* had a wide readership. Its national circulation initiated the establishment of Houses of Hospitality across the country.

a salary. The entire operation depended on donations, and as soon as any money came in, bills were paid and anything left over went to the poor. "A great many of our friends urge us to put our paper on a businesslike basis," Day wrote in the paper in 1934. "But this isn't a business, it's a movement. . . . Each time we have asked for aid, the money was immediately forthcoming to pay each and every bill. True, this leaves nothing for the next printing bill. . . . God seems to intend us to depend solely on Him. . . . Economic security . . . is not for us. We must live by faith, from day to day."[10]

So did many of their neighbors. The Catholic Workers lived in a tenement, in one of New York City's poorest neighborhoods, and they first opened their doors during the depths of the Great Depression, when millions of Americans were out of work and desperately poor. Destitute men came to the New York House of Hospitality looking for warm clothes. "They are without coats, many of them without underwear," Day wrote in the mid-1930s. "Their feet show bare through the cracks in their shoes. We haven't even women's sweaters to give them."

"We didn't have any intention of starting a coffee line. When we didn't have clothes we invited the men to have a cup of coffee. With the cold weather the group has grown steadily larger."[11] Eventually, hundreds showed up each morning for coffee and bread. Some came back for soup at lunch and dinnertime as well.

Over the years, Catholic Workers were often arrested at prolabor and antiwar demonstrations. (Day's last trip to jail came when she was in her seventies, during the summer of 1973, in support of a campaign by Cesar Chavez's United Farmworkers Union to improve the lives of migrant farmworkers in California.) In 1934, Catholic Workers joined Communist-organized strikers picketing Ohrbach's, a New York department store. Day later wrote:

> The fact that Communists made issue of Negro exploitation and labor trouble was no reason why we should stay out of the situation. "The truth is the truth," writes St. Thomas, "and proceeds from the Holy Ghost, no matter from whose lips it comes."
>
> There was mass picketing every Saturday afternoon during the Ohrbach strike, and every Saturday the police drove up with patrol wagons and loaded the pickets into them with their banners and took them to jail. When we entered the dispute with our slogans drawn from the writings of the popes regarding the condition of labor, the police around Union Square were taken aback and did not know what to do. It was as though they were arresting the Holy Father himself, one of them said, were they to load our pickets and their signs into their patrol wagons. The police contented themselves with giving us all injunctions.[12]

Through the hard times of the 1930s, the Catholic Worker movement grew by leaps and bounds. Circulation of *The Catholic Worker* grew to 185,000 nationwide by the end of the decade.[13] Inspired by the newspaper and by Day and Maurin's tireless travels speaking for the movement, locally controlled

Houses of Hospitality sprang up in cities across the country. Several farming communes were started.

The movement attracted droves of volunteers—idealistic young people who typically served only briefly as well as older Workers drawn from among those served by the movement. The movement, Day once wrote, "is, in a way, a school, a work camp, to which large-hearted, socially conscious young people come to find their vocations. After some months or years, they know most definitely what they want to do with their lives. Some go into medicine, nursing, law, teaching, farming, writing, and publishing."[14]

The way the Workers saw it, all gave and all received. Workers received gifts of God's grace through giving to others, and sought to transform themselves spiritually while transforming society.

Blessed are the Peacemakers

The Catholic Worker movement had, from the beginning, been opposed to war in all its forms. During World War II, Day wrote: "We are still pacifists. Our manifesto is the Sermon on the Mount, which means that we will try to be peacemakers. . . . We will not participate in armed warfare or in making munitions, or by buying government bonds to prosecute the war, or in urging others to these efforts."[15]

The Workers' opposition to the war, together with the general wartime improvement in the nation's economy (which meant fewer people out of work), cut into public support for the Catholic Worker movement. By 1948, Day wrote in a journal she kept that year, there were only eleven Houses of

Hospitality and farms nationwide, down from an earlier high of thirty-two.

Around this time, the movement also suffered the loss of one of its two founders. Peter Maurin died in 1949, but he had stopped his teaching and talking after having been disabled by a stroke five years earlier. "I can no longer think," he said. And so he had become mostly silent.

After World War II, Catholic Workers continued to work for peace. Through the 1950s and into the 1960s, they focused much of their attention on stopping the nuclear arms race. In the mid- to late 1950s, for example, Catholic Workers were arrested for refusing to participate in air-raid drills, during which all residents of the area included in the drill were required by law to take shelter as they would be expected to do in case of a nuclear attack. In the 1960s, they opposed the Vietnam War.

Catholic Workers also supported the civil-rights movement in the 1950s and 1960s. "After so many years of work in the Peace Movement," Day wrote in 1963, "I had come to the conclusion that basic to peace was this struggle of the colored for education, job opportunity, health, and recognition as human beings."[16]

Seeing Christ in Others

But the Workers never abandoned their mission to serve the poor. "As long as men keep coming to the door," Day wrote in 1972, "we will keep on preparing each day the food they need."[17]

Since the Depression years of the 1930s, though, the kinds of people served by the Houses of Hospitality had changed. During the Depression, the soup

By 1961, when this picture was taken, Dorothy Day and the Catholic Workers had become involved with the civil-rights struggles of the day.

lines were filled with ordinary working people for whom no work could be found. After the economy improved, a large proportion of those served by the Workers were not merely unemployed but unemployable—drunks, drug addicts, the mentally ill and physically disabled.

The Catholic Workers' generous hospitality was often rewarded with curses and violence. "We learned (and it was painful)," one Worker said, "that if you gave the poor man your coat he was just as likely to hit you on the head and steal your pants."[18] But the Workers persisted in following their religious mandate to serve those in need, no matter what the reason for their poverty. The Workers tried to see Christ in everyone.

"What else do we all want," Day explained, "each one of us, except to love and be loved, in our families, in our work, in all our relationships? God is Love. Love casts out fear. . . . When you love people, you see all the good in them, all the Christ in them. God sees Christ, his Son, in us. And so we should see Christ in others, *and nothing else,* and love them. There can never be enough of it."[19]

Perhaps the most lasting legacy of the Catholic Worker movement has been in training and inspiring Workers, the people they have served, mainstream Catholics, and even non-Catholic social activists to "see Christ in others" and to take Catholic spirituality into the world of social action. Through the movement's ties to diverse public servants, peace activists, and advocates for the poor, its influence has permeated generations of American social activism. And all, Day wrote, by the grace of God:

"We were just sitting there talking when Peter Maurin came in.

"We were just sitting there talking when lines of people began to form, saying, 'We need bread.' . . . There was always bread.

"We were just sitting there talking and people moved in on us. . . . And somehow the walls expanded. . . .

"It was as casual as that, I often think. It just came about. It just happened. . . .

"The most significant thing about the Catholic Worker is poverty, some say.

"The most significant thing is community, others say. We are not alone anymore.

"But the final word is love. . . . We cannot love God unless we love each other. We know Him in the breaking of bread, and we know each other in the breaking of bread, and we are not alone anymore. . . ."

"We have all known the long loneliness and we have learned that the only solution is love and that love comes with community.

"It all happened while we sat there talking, and it is still going on."[20]

Dorothy Day died in 1980. The Catholic Worker movement, though much reduced in numbers since its heyday in the 1930s, has continued without her. Houses of Hospitality still serve the poor.

At a convention in February 1965, a Nation of Islam leader preaches that Malcolm X, a former Nation leader who later denounced the separatist practices of the organization, had gotten what he deserved when he was assassinated a few days earlier.

NATION OF ISLAM

"CHRISTIANITY IS THE WHITE MAN'S RELIGION. . . .
[THE BIBLE] AND HIS INTERPRETATIONS OF IT, HAVE
BEEN THE GREATEST SINGLE IDEOLOGICAL WEAPON
FOR ENSLAVING MILLIONS OF NON-WHITE HUMAN
BEINGS."

— MALCOLM X[1]

Partly derived from the religion of Islam, partly a
black separatist social, economic, and political movement, the Nation of Islam has been controversial—
angry, divisive, uncompromising—since its
beginnings in the 1930s. Under the leadership of
Louis Farrakhan, the Nation of Islam today is more
controversial than ever.

Early Years

In Detroit in 1930, Elijah (or perhaps Robert) Poole,
the son of Baptist Georgia sharecroppers, former
slaves, met a peddler and preacher named Wali Farad
Muhammad. According to his followers, Farad was

"Allah in person." Convinced, Poole changed his name to Elijah Muhammad, and when Farad mysteriously disappeared in 1934, Elijah Muhammad dedicated the rest of his life to preaching Farad's "revelation" and founding the Nation of Islam, a new and unique version of Islam.

The central and defining belief of the Nation of Islam (also known as the Black Muslims), as taught by Elijah Muhammad, was that black people from the time of their creation had been Allah's "chosen people." White people were "devils" originally created by Yacub, a mad black scientist. For thousands of years the white race had ruled the black race—but this time of oppression would soon end, when the white race destroyed itself through war.

The mission of the Nation of Islam, then, was to prepare black people to inherit the earth and live free. To accomplish this, the Nation encouraged black people to create their own separate, self-sufficient, and self-reliant communities and to observe a strict and disciplined moral code based on the laws of Islam.

Elijah Muhammad called himself Allah's "Messenger" to the "Lost-Found Nation of Islam in the Wilderness of North America." In contrast to the black Christian churches, which were rooted most strongly in the rural South, the Nation of Islam found most of its converts among poor blacks in the urban North. Many converts to the Nation of Islam were found in prison, and the extraordinary effect the Nation had on the lives of convicts earned widespread approval in many black communities. Young men who had gone into prison as thieves and gangsters came out clean-cut and clean-shaved, neatly dressed, abstaining from drugs, alcohol, and tobacco, and fiercely motivated to live better lives.

Malcolm X

The Nation's most famous prison convert was Malcolm Little. In 1952, in a Massachusetts state prison, this drug dealer, pimp, and thief took Elijah Muhammad's message to heart and transformed himself. Dropping his "slave name," he became Malcolm X.

When Malcolm got out of prison, he dedicated his life to the Nation of Islam. He became a minister, and his passionate, angry, intensely personal preaching in the 1950s and early 1960s attracted many converts. The Nation of Islam grew from a small group of only a few hundred followers of Elijah Muhammad to a national movement with ten thousand or more members.

Malcolm's fiery rhetoric contrasted sharply with the words of such civil-rights leaders and black Christian preachers as Martin Luther King, Jr. King believed in the transformative power of nonviolence, and he worked toward a colorblind, racially integrated, tolerant America offering equal opportunity to all of its citizens.

Malcolm, on the other hand, was militant and uncompromisingly antiwhite. Instead of seeking integration, he urged black Americans to create a separate world for themselves: "We don't want to integrate with that ole pale thing!" he said. "The dog is their closest relative. They got the same kind of hair, the same kind of skin, and the same kind of *smell!*"[2]

In 1964, however, Malcolm separated from the Nation of Islam. The chief reason for his break, it seems, was his discovery that Elijah Muhammad—contrary to the Nation's strict forbidding of sex outside of marriage—had had sexual relationships with a series of young women serving as his secretaries. This truly shocked Malcolm. "I had discovered Muslims had been betrayed by Elijah Muhammad himself," he later said.[3]

Malcolm spoke out about this "betrayal" both to other Black Muslims and to the press. In response, the Nation of Islam cast Malcolm out of the church.

While this conflict between Malcolm and the Nation was playing out, Malcolm was also undergoing a great personal, spiritual change. In the spring of 1964, Malcolm had made a pilgrimage alone to Mecca, the spiritual center of Islam, in Saudi Arabia. (Islam mandates that all Muslims should, if at all possible, visit Mecca at least once in their lives.) On a plane filled with fellow pilgrims, "white, black, brown, red, and yellow people, blue eyes and blond hair, and my kinky red hair—all together, brothers . . . ," he later recalled, "the feeling hit me that there really wasn't any color problem here." When he finally reached Mecca, he said, it was "the first time I had ever stood before the Creator of All and felt like a complete human being."[4]

Malcolm's pilgrimage to Mecca started in him a process of spiritual transformation, moving him toward a more mainstream and inclusive Islam, away from the unorthodox religious peculiarities of the Nation, and away from his previously hostile black separatism. When he returned home, he announced at an airport press conference that his pilgrimage had

Malcolm Little, who became known as Malcolm X, was the most famous prison convert of the Nation of Islam. He later grew disillusioned with the church and felt betrayed by its founder, Elijah Muhammad.

made him a new man: "In the past, yes, I have made sweeping indictments of *all* white people," he said. "I will never be guilty of that again. . . . A blanket indictment of all white people is as wrong as when whites make blanket indictments against blacks."[5] With great difficulty, Malcolm set about re-creating himself—his religious beliefs, his prescriptions for black America, his ministry.

The Nation of Islam attacked him viciously and relentlessly. Many of his fellow ministers had long resented Malcolm's fame, and the Nation's leadership now encouraged them to denounce him. One particularly prominent spokeman for the Nation at this time was a young minister who had been brought into the Nation by Malcolm himself—Louis Farrakhan. In December 1964, in a Nation of Islam newspaper, Farrakhan wrote: "Only those who wish to be led to hell, or to their doom, will follow Malcolm. The die is set and Malcolm shall not escape. . . . Such a man as Malcolm is worthy of death."[6]

Frightening rhetoric such as this from the Nation's leaders—as well as direct threats from some of their followers—convinced Malcolm that he was going to die. On February 21, 1965, Malcolm X was shot to death while speaking to a rally at the Audubon Ballroom in Harlem. Three Black Muslims were convicted of killing him.

Black Nationalism and the Nation of Islam

The Nation of Islam from its beginning has been not only a religious movement but also a branch of a social/political tradition known as black nationalism.

Black nationalism (which has been around in one form or another for as long as there have been black people in North America) holds that African Americans must organize together and build just and prosperous communities for themselves, without much assistance from white people. Black nationalism sometimes takes the form of black separatism—the conviction that blacks must build their nation in their own, physically separate territory. The Nation of Islam preaches black separatism.

Before the Nation, though, there was Marcus Garvey. Born in Jamaica, Garvey founded the Universal Negro Improvement Association, dedicated to promoting unity and betterment among blacks worldwide, in 1914. Convinced that blacks living in white-majority countries such as the United States would always be oppressed, Garvey encouraged a "back to Africa" movement, in which a homeland would be created in Africa for black emigrants. Garvey was enormously influential among black Americans in the 1920s—until his conviction for misuse of his supporters' funds got him deported to Jamaica.

Where black separatism is concerned, the Nation of Islam picked up where Garvey left off. Although spokesmen for the Nation have sometimes talked about an African state, the organization's preference from the beginning has been that the U.S. government should set aside land within the country's borders for a separate African-American nation. According to a 1995 Nation of Islam publication: "We want our people in America whose parents or grandparents were descendant from slaves, to be allowed to establish a separate state or territory of their own—

either on this continent or elsewhere. We believe that our former slave masters are obligated to provide such land and that the area must be fertile and minerally rich."[7]

The Nation of Islam has also inspired other black nationalists. In the late 1960s and early 1970s, especially, black nationalist revolutionaries including the Black Panthers took inspiration from the Nation's emphasis on black pride and solidarity in general, and from the fiery rhetoric of Malcolm X in particular.

Louis Farrakhan

In 1975, Elijah Muhammad died and his son, W. Deen Muhammad, took over the leadership of the Nation of Islam. By then, the Nation claimed more than 50,000 members and (in pursuit of Elijah Muhammad's goal of economic independence) commanded a business empire worth tens of millions of dollars. The younger Muhammad changed the organization's name (to World Community of Al-Islam in the West) and sought to move his flock into the mainstream of the world's Muslims. He also moved away from black separatism and opened his organization to people of all races.

Most Black Muslims made "the change" (as they called it) with their new leader. Several thousand of them did not, however, preferring instead to remain true to the teachings of Elijah Muhammad. Their leader was Louis Farrakhan.

In the late 1970s and early 1980s, Farrakhan crisscrossed the country, speaking to countless crowds and recruiting young men for the Fruit of Islam, an elite service corps for the Nation. In 1984, he became nationally known among white as well as black Americans through his energetic, high-profile backing of Jesse Jackson's campaign for the presidency.

With greater publicity came closer public scrutiny and criticism. Farrakhan has been widely criticized for his persistent antiwhite racism in general, and for his verbal attacks on Jews in particular. For example, in a speech recorded in October 1995, Farrakhan said: "Many of the Jews who owned the homes, the apartments in the black community, we considered them bloodsuckers because they took from our community and built their community. But they didn't offer anything back to the community. And when the Jews left, the Palestinian Arabs came, Koreans came, Vietnamese and other ethnic and racial groups came. And so this is a type, and we call them bloodsuckers."[8]

Under Farrakhan's leadership, the Nation has sought to expand its business empire by investing in farmland, restaurants, hair- and skin-care products, and banking and insurance enterprises. In addition (and in a clear departure from the Nation's earlier economic separatism), by the early 1990s the Nation was seeking contracts with federal, state, and local governments (mostly for providing security for public housing) and with white-owned businesses.

Also in the early 1990s, Farrakhan began reaching out to other organizations of black Americans. In 1995 he organized a "Million Man March" on Washington. Some mainstream black leaders, including former NAACP head Benjamin Chavis, signed on as supporters of the march. Many others, citing

Farrakhan's long history of strident intolerance, refused to be associated with him.

Ultimately, on October 16, 1995, at least half a million African Americans gathered in Washington. Although the Million Man March didn't seek to include white people, a few white onlookers were present. Only black men were invited—black women were asked to stay home. Unlike past civil-rights marches, which demanded equality, opportunity, and freedom, the 1995 march and Farrakhan, its keynote speaker, made most of its demands on the marchers, insisting that they should take more responsibility for themselves and their families and their black communities.

The most powerful feature of the Million Man March turned out to be not Louis Farrakhan, but the marchers themselves. Peaceful, relaxed, and courteous, the hundreds of thousands of marchers had their minds on brotherhood and personal growth. When they left, they hoped to bring that spirit home with them. "I'm not here for Farrakhan," one marcher said. "I'm here to be a proud black man."[9]

Islam and the Nation of Islam

The Nation of Islam is, and always has been, well outside of the mainstream of the religion of Islam. Its teachings differ sharply in some respects from orthodox Islam. Most notably, Islam teaches that there is only one God, Allah, and that Allah's last messenger was the Prophet Mohammad. The Nation of Islam teaches not only that Wali Farad was a living incarnation of Allah (much as Christians believe of Jesus) but also that Elijah Muhammad was his mes-

Practitioners of mainstream Islam are an ever-growing presence in this country. Here a worshiper, facing Mecca, pauses to pray.

senger, whose teachings carry the same kind of authority as the Prophet Mohammad's.

Orthodox Islam also does not subscribe to the racist teachings of the Nation. It embraces all races and does not advocate racial separatism; nor does it agree with the Nation of Islam that blacks are Allah's "chosen people" and that whites are devils.

In the 1980s and early 1990s, the number of Muslims in America rose sharply, to about 3 or 4 million. Of these, only a small minority belonged to the Nation of Islam. About two thirds of American Muslims in the early 1990s were immigrants or children of immigrants, mostly from the Arab world or from such Asian nations as Pakistan. The remaining one third were American-born converts, most of them black. Perhaps 20,000 of these black American Muslims belonged to the Nation of Islam.[10]

Most American Muslims follow a strict personal moral code, as do members of the Nation of Islam. Their religious obligations include: facing Mecca and praying five times each day, observing dietary restrictions (including no pork or alcohol), abstaining from gambling, and adhering to strict sexual standards (including modest clothes and no sex outside of marriage). Most American converts to either the Nation or a more conventional version of Islam also take Muslim names as a sign of their new faith.

By the mid-1990s, many American Muslims were reexamining the role of women in Islam, insisting that many restrictions placed on women in Islamic countries come from their culture, not from the Koran (Islam's sacred scripture). Similar discussions about the permissible roles and religious obligations of women were under way among Christians (including Mormons) and Jews as well as Muslims, with widely differing results in various branches of the faiths. The Nation of Islam has generally been quite conservative and restrictive where women are concerned, for example requiring them to wear long skirts or pants and to cover their heads in public. On the other hand, it has also allowed some women to become ministers, a role most of the Islamic world has reserved for men alone.

Black Americans and the Nation of Islam

It is difficult to measure the Nation's influence among black Americans. Estimates of Nation of Islam membership in the early 1990s ranged from fewer than 10,000 to as many as 100,000.[11] However, the Nation's actual membership statistics undoubtedly understate its influence. Many black American Muslims not currently in the Nation were first attracted to their religion through the Nation of Islam. In addition, many black Americans who don't believe in the Nation's theology nonetheless warmly support its message of black solidarity and self-respect, and the disciplined behavior it has encouraged in black youth. Many are reluctant to criticize any strong black voice—even Farrakhan's, even when they disagree with him.

Most black Americans, however, are not racial separatists. Most support the ideal of a racially integrated and tolerant society. Many also believe that Farrakhan's focus on self-help and individual responsibility comes too close to blaming the black victims of racism in America for their plight and absolving white Americans from any responsibility for their black fellow citizens.

The Nation of Islam, since its beginnings in the 1930s, has had its strongest appeal during hard times for black Americans. And during the 1980s and 1990s, conditions in black inner-city communities (where the Nation is strongest) have grown worse and worse. "There are a lot of frustrated, angry, bitter people who are looking for a leader," a black congressman from Brooklyn explains. "In some cases they are looking for something to hate."[12]

LUBAVITCHER HASIDIM

"LIKE ALL JEWS, I'M HERE FOR A PURPOSE. TO SEE
THE BEAUTY AND HOLINESS IN EVERYDAY THINGS.
TO TRY TO ELEVATE ORDINARY LIFE. THE KEY IS IN
THE TORAH [JEWISH SCRIPTURE], AND THE WAY TO
GET THERE HAS BEEN SHOWN US IN A PRACTICAL
WAY BY THE *MITZVOT* [THE 613 COMMANDMENTS
OBSERVED BY ORTHODOX JEWS WHICH GOVERN EV-
ERY ASPECT OF THEIR LIVES]."
                              — A LUBAVITCHER WOMAN[1]

The Lubavitchers, a group of Hasidic Jews, have created a community for themselves that is visibly very
separate from the secular world—clustering together
in close-knit neighborhoods, sending their children
to private religious schools, wearing distinctive dress,
eating in their own restaurants, shopping in their own
stores. Yet they have persistently reached out to less-
observant Jews, and welcomed *baalei teshuva* ("those
who have returned") into their fold. From a tiny rem-
nant of Holocaust survivors, they have grown to
number perhaps a quarter of a million worldwide
today.

Lubavitcher families live in close-knit communities and separate themselves from the secular world, most obviously through their style of dress.

From Eastern Europe to America

Modern Hasidism began in the 1700s with Rabbi Israel ben Eliezer, an eastern European Jewish scholar
and teacher better known today as the Baal Shem
Tov ("master of the good name"), or Besht. Instead
of limiting himself to the dry and remote language
of scholars, the Baal Shem Tov taught with stories
and parables that brought traditional Jewish learn-
ing and mysticism within reach of the unlearned
majority of Jews. His message that even the lowli-
est of Jews could draw closer to God through joy-
fully devoting themselves to holiness in everyday
life—in eating and drinking, praying and dancing
and singing, making love and raising a family—
proved to be powerfully appealing. In the 1800s, the
majority of Jews in central and eastern Europe came
to embrace Hasidism.

The leaders of this movement modeled themselves on the Baal Shem Tov, creating the institution
of the charismatic *tzaddik* ("righteous man") or *rebbe*
(Yiddish for "rabbi" or "teacher"). A Hasidic rebbe's
followers seek to consult him on every important decision in their lives, from whom they should marry
to where they should live and what jobs they should
pursue. The rebbe is the exclusive spiritual leader of
his flock, not only a teacher and spiritual father but
also an intermediary between his followers and God.
(This contrasts sharply with other forms of Judaism,
in which rabbis are respected as learned teachers but
are not seen as being somehow closer to God than
other Jews.)

Each rebbe typically has passed his authority—
and his followers—on to a spiritual heir, usually a
son or son-in-law. In this manner, each dynastic line

of rebbes has become associated with generations of followers, known as their court. Hasidic courts are named after the town or region where they first thrived, and thus the Lubavitcher Hasidim are named after the Russian town of Lubavitch.

Hasidim and other central and eastern European Jews endured terrible persecution in the nineteenth and twentieth centuries, culminating in the Nazi Holocaust. Many Hasidic courts were entirely wiped out. Others emigrated, much reduced in number, mostly to America and what is now Israel. And there they have stayed. Followers of a half dozen Hasidic courts have enclaves in the New York area today; of these, the Lubavitchers are by far the most visible and outgoing.

In 1940 the sixth Lubavitcher rebbe, Yosef Schneersohn, fled Nazi-occupied Poland and moved as much of his court as he could save to Crown Heights, a middle-class neighborhood in Brooklyn, New York. The rebbe's daughter Chaya Moussia and her husband, the scholarly and pious Rabbi Menachem Mendel Schneerson (a distant cousin), escaped safely in 1941. Another daughter and her entire family perished in 1942 at the Treblinka concentration camp.

Safe in Crown Heights, the rebbe set about rebuilding his community, transplanting its eastern European customs and rigorous observance of Jewish law into the fertile ground of America.

What Do Lubavitchers Believe?

First and foremost, Lubavitchers believe in meticulously performing the *mitzvot*, commandments that range from prohibitions against murder and adultery to dietary (kosher) laws and detailed instructions for observing the Sabbath. On the Sabbath, for example, which begins at sundown on Friday and continues through Saturday, all work is forbidden—even driving a car to synagogue. Far from feeling restricted by this, Lubavitchers say that they look forward to the Sabbath all week. "I feel that I'm getting a break," said one woman who commonly cooks in advance and then enjoys Sabbath meals with a half dozen or more family and friends. "What if you were flown to a quiet tropical island every week? Wouldn't you be pleased if you were permitted—even obliged—to put aside your everyday burdens and chores? . . . I doubt if most [nonobservant] families get the chance we do just to sit around and talk to each other every weekend."[2]

The primary reason for performing *mitzvot* is simply because God has commanded it. For Hasidim, performing *mitzvot* is a joyful, satisfying, all-encompassing way of life. Furthermore, Hasidim believe that the performance of each and every *mitzvah*, no matter how mundane, brings the world closer to the state of harmony and holiness that will make it possible for the Messiah (*Moshiach* in Yiddish, the preferred language of Lubavitchers) to appear on Earth, restoring the world to Garden of Eden perfection. Thus, Hasidim believe (and Lubavitchers are especially fervent in this belief) that the redemption of all of humankind depends upon Jews scrupulously observing God's commandments. "There is a saying among Hasidim," a Lubavitcher man in Crown Heights noted, "that the Messiah will come 'when the wellsprings of the Baal Shem Tov spread out,' . . . when everything he taught becomes the common practice of all Jews."[3]

Many Hasidic communities, much like the Amish, hold themselves apart from the outside world and don't proselytize. But the Lubavitchers vigorously pursue a mission of convincing as many Jews as possible to perform as many *mitzvot* as possible. "*Mitzvah* tanks"—vans filled with young Lubavitchers—cruise towns and cities across the United States, seeking out less-observant Jews to offer them fellowship and urge them to perform *mitzvot*.

Women and Men

Hasidic men and women in many ways live in separate worlds. A Hasidic man is forbidden to so much as touch a woman other than his wife, not even to shake hands. (He may not even touch *his wife* in public.) Men and women sit in separate sections in Hasidic as in all Orthodox Jewish synagogues, to avoid opposite-sex distractions from the religious business at hand. Men and women dance in separate rooms at Lubavitcher weddings. There simply is no opportunity in Lubavitcher life for the kind of nonsexual friendships common among men and women in the secular world.

Every Lubavitcher is expected to seek marriage and a family. There is no Jewish spiritual tradition of celibacy, no Jewish nuns or celibate priests. When a young Lubavitcher reaches a marriageable age, friends of the family (or perhaps a matchmaker) will recommend possible partners. Young people are encouraged to decide within a few dates whether they are suitable for marriage, and they do decide for themselves. Women as well as men can reject proposed marriage partners. However, there is considerable pressure to find a partner and settle down. "A single person is only a half of a person," a women's dean at a Lubavitcher school pointed out in the late 1980s. "People are incomplete unless they are married."[4]

To modern American eyes, the separate world of Hasidic women seems inferior. Women may not become rabbis. Women are expected to pursue less education than men. Women are expected to bear many children, and in practice this means that much of their time is consumed by child-rearing and housekeeping. (There is no prohibition against women working outside the home, but—as it is for men—work in the secular world is seen as a means to an end, a way to earn money to support their family and community, rather than a satisfying end in itself.)

However, through Hasidic eyes the world looks quite different. "Any hint of inferior status" for women is, according to a Lubavitcher publication, "not a result of Torah law, but a reflection of the times and culture."[5] Hasidim respect and value the role of women in taking care of home and family because home and family—not the synagogue, and certainly not success in the outside world—are central to Hasidic spiritual and social life. Taking care of one's family is an absolute obligation. Elderly Lubavitchers, for example, typically live with their relatives rather than in retirement communities. Home and family (and especially children) are to be protected and kept separate from the secular world, and for their central role in accomplishing this women are valued and respected.

A good example of how things look different to Hasidic and modern American eyes is the ritual bath (*mikvah*). According to Jewish law, the *mikvah* is a ritual not to remove dirtiness (the person going into the *mikvah* washes beforehand) but to change spiritual status. It prepares one to perform certain holy functions. Hasidic men immerse themselves at a *mikvah* before performing certain Sabbath *mitzvot*. Hasidic wives (not unmarried women) immerse themselves before resuming sexual relations with their husbands seven days after menstruation, to prepare themselves spiritually for sex.

For sex, in the world of the Orthodox, is holy. This is partly because sex involves the possibility of conceiving a child. (Birth control is not practiced in most circumstances by Hasidim, in large part as a conscious effort to make up for the loss of so many Jews in the Holocaust with the birth of many Jewish children.) In addition, though, joyful sex between husband and wife is itself holy and blessed by God (even and perhaps especially on the Sabbath), and both husband and wife are expected to seek one another's pleasure.

Similarly, the prohibition against husbands and wives touching each other or otherwise displaying affection in public has to do not with sex being somehow dirty, but instead with it being intensely private. Hasidim feel that this privateness, the wall of modesty around sex, makes tenderness and touching especially charged with emotion and eroticism. So, they say, does the period of required abstinence during and after menstruation each month, which in addition may discourage men from taking their wives for granted as always-available playthings.

The Seventh Rebbe

In 1950 the Rebbe Yosef Schneersohn died, after a decade of ambitious efforts not only to establish the Lubavitcher community in Crown Heights but also

Menachem Mendel Schneerson became the Lubavitchers' seventh rebbe in 1951. His influence was so great that following his death in 1994, no new rebbe was chosen. Lubavitchers remain divided as to whether he was the Messiah.

to aid Jews around the world and to reach out to less-observant American Jews, educating them and encouraging them to live by Jewish law. It was clear to the entire community who the rebbe's successor should be: his forty-eight-year-old son-in-law Menachem Mendel Schneerson.

Menachem Mendel Schneerson since childhood had been known as a brilliant student of Jewish law and literature. Very unusual among Lubavitchers, who usually eschew secular education, he had earned a degree at a prestigious secular university (the Sorbonne, in Paris). At his father-in-law's request, he had organized several Lubavitcher publishing, social service, and outreach missions based in Crown Heights but with a wide-ranging reach across America and even overseas. Widely respected for his wisdom and piety, the white-bearded, sky-blue-eyed Schneerson also possessed the qualities of a charismatic leader. In 1951 he became the Lubavitchers' seventh rebbe.

For decades, Lubavitchers and even outsiders who respected the Rebbe Schneerson's wisdom and holiness lined up each week on Sunday morning at his home. One by one, he would listen to their stories and requests, and offer them advice, blessings, and a single dollar bill each, to be given to charity.

The rebbe continued his predecessor's aggressive outreach in the United States and around the world, wherever there were communities with sizable numbers of Jews—from Canada to South America to South Africa, as well as in Europe and Israel, Australia, and even Asia. Lubavitchers took particular interest in the plight of Jews in the former Soviet Union, and in helping them to emigrate. Since the breakup of the Soviet Union, Lubavitchers have worked to establish services and build synagogues for Jews who wish to remain there.

But Lubavitchers have remained most active in the United States. On college campuses, Chabad Houses have offered Sabbath dinners and services to young Jews living away from home. Several dozen *yeshivas* (religious schools) have been established around the country. So have summer camps, attended by tens of thousands of children each year. By the early 1990s, there were about 1,500 Lubavitcher outposts—schools, camps, synagogues, and other centers—worldwide, with most of them in the United States.[6]

Since mid-century, the number of Lubavitchers has doubled about every ten years, so that by the mid-1990s there were perhaps a quarter of a million of them worldwide (making them the largest of the Hasidic courts today), with 15,000 to 20,000 living in Crown Heights. This phenomenal increase has been partly due to the Lubavitchers' extremely high birth-rate—half a dozen or more children per family is common—and the fact that so many of their children remain Lubavitchers as adults. "Calculating conservatively," one Orthodox mother of 14 has written, "I may have 100 grandchildren, become great-grandmother to 1,000 and live to embrace some great-great-grandchildren."[7] In addition, a surprising number of Lubavitchers—likely more than half in recent years—are *baalei teshuva*, those who chose this way of life as adults.[8]

While the Lubavitcher community was thriving, its rebbe's neighborhood was not. Crown Heights has long been an ethnic mix, including an increasing

The death of a black child after a car in a Lubavitcher motorcade accidentally struck him in Crown Heights, Brooklyn, in 1991 incited days of anti-Jewish rioting. Relations between Lubavitchers and their African-American neighbors have been uneasy ever since.

number of middle-class and wealthier blacks in the 1950s. In the 1960s, poorer people, mostly black, moved in and crime increased. Many of those who could afford it—black as well as white—moved to the suburbs, but not the Lubavitchers. Their rebbe decided to stay, and so did they. Relations between the Lubavitchers and many of their black neighbors deteriorated through the 1960s, 1970s, and 1980s.

Then, in August 1991, a car in the rebbe's motorcade went out of control and struck and killed a black child. Crown Heights erupted into days of anti-Jewish rioting. That night, a young Hasidic scholar from Australia was stabbed to death. Relations between Lubavitchers and African Americans in Crown Heights have simmered ever since.

Moshiach Is Coming?

There's a long Jewish tradition that each generation has its own potential Messiah. (Moses was one, for example, but the Israelites' sinfulness prevented him from actually becoming the Messiah.) Jewish tradition also holds that the Messiah will come after a great cataclysm. Both the sixth and the seventh Lubavitcher rebbes believed that the Holocaust had been such a cataclysm, and that the Messiah could therefore arrive very soon—as soon as enough Jews followed God's laws well enough to make the world habitable for the Messiah.

The Rebbe Schneerson suffered a heart attack in 1978, but recovered. In March 1992, he was gravely disabled by a stroke. He could no longer speak, and could communicate only through such small and cryptic gestures as tilting his head, moving his hand, lifting an eyebrow. Interpreting these signals, his aides divined when he was feeling well enough to appear in public, then summoned the faithful to the synagogue. (Many Lubavitcher men took to wearing beepers so they wouldn't miss an appearance.)

For the year or so before his stroke, the rebbe had not effectively discouraged (and sometimes seemed actually to encourage) speculation among his followers that he would himself soon be revealed as the Messiah. After he became disabled, his followers read what they wished into his gestures. At every appearance, huge crowds greeted their ailing rebbe, singing and dancing and chanting: We want Moshiach NOW! A division grew among his followers, between those convinced that the rebbe was the Messiah, and those who did not believe that the Messiah's time had yet come.

The rebbe died on June 12, 1994. He named no successor before he died, and he had no children and no uniquely close spiritual protégé. Several years after his death, the Lubavitchers had chosen no new rebbe. And they remained divided about whether Menachem Mendel Schneerson was the Messiah.

Lubavitchers and Other American Jews

Lubavitchers would prefer that all Jews accept their entire way of life but nonetheless see each and every *mitzvah* performed as something to be celebrated. And so they have willingly provided information useful for less-observant Jews interested in observing only some of the religious laws. For example, many non-Lubavitchers check Friday's newspaper for the regular advertisement run by the Lubavitchers noting the time (which varies) that Sabbath candles should be lit that evening.

Many American Jews are ambivalent about the Lubavitchers. In some ways, their ambivalence is similar to what many assimilated Americans feel about more-recent immigrants from their homelands—nostalgia for a lost way of life and affection for one's ancestors mixed with embarrassment at how foreign, how unassimilated they are. But there's also a purely religious ambivalence at work: Lubavitchers seem so authentically and scrupulously Jewish, so confident and joyful in their faith that other Jews can look at them and feel proud about being Jewish and at the same time feel guilty about not being observant enough. And many, perhaps most, Jews have been uncomfortable with the cult of personality that developed around the Rebbe Menachem Mendel Schneerson.

Still, much of the money donated to the Lubavitchers (the organization by 1990 was taking in an estimated $100 million in contributions each year)[9] has come from less-observant Jews, many perhaps seeking to keep alive the kind of religion practiced by their parents and grandparents, even if they have felt unable to practice it themselves. In an uncertain world, where so many Americans feel insecure, the Lubavitchers offer certainty: clearly defined roles for men and women, stable family life, and an unambiguous path to God. In its language and manner of dress and many other customs, the Lubavitcher sect also keeps alive elements of a *culture*—eastern European Jewish culture—that was destroyed in its homeland by the Holocaust but is nonetheless part of the heritage of most American Jews.

QUAKERS

"ABOVE ALL, WE REMAIN OPEN TO WHERE GOD'S
SPIRIT WILL LEAD US."
— FRIENDS COMMITTEE ON
NATIONAL LEGISLATION[1]

Coming out of the same Protestant religious ferment
that gave rise to the Amish in Europe, the Quakers
took a very different path. Far from separating themselves from the world, they've remained very much
engaged in it. Their most far-reaching gift to the rest
of us has thus been their persistent and practical service to society.

Early Quakers

Quakerism began with the preaching of George Fox,
a weaver's son, in northern England. Uncomfortable
with the established religions of his time, Fox
struggled throughout his youth to resolve his religious yearnings until, in his early twenties, he experienced a series of spiritual insights. Feeling

Quakerism, or the Society of Friends, began in England from a background similar to the Amish in Europe.

compelled to share these insights with others, he spoke out and was imprisoned for blasphemy during the winter months of 1650-1651. After he was released from jail, Fox traveled over the English countryside, preaching. One woman who heard him speak and was deeply impressed wrote that Fox "opened us a book we had never read in, . . . the Light of Christ in our consciences, and . . . declared of it that it was our teacher."[2]

"Stand still in the Light," Fox wrote, "and submit to it, and the temptations and troubles will be hushed and gone: and then content comes from the Lord, and help contrary to your expectation. Then ye grow up in peace."[3] Beginning in 1652, Fox's teachings sparked a spiritual revival, winning hundreds of converts to his views.

Fox, like many of the radical dissenting Protestants across Europe in those times, appealed strongly to the poor and oppressed, offering them a vision of a pure Christian fellowship in which all believers were equal. "Quaker" was originally a label used by enemies, mocking the believers' religious fervor. Fox and his followers called themselves "Children of Light" and, as they are known today, the "Society of Friends."

Quakers believe that every person who seeks it has access to the "Light of God" and with this inner light can discern spiritual truth. At the heart of the Quaker religious experience is the unique Quaker meeting for worship, at which Friends gather together, sit in silence, and listen for God's leading. Any member of the group who feels led by God to do so during the meeting will stand and speak a message or offer a prayer. There is no liturgy, no creed, no sacrament, no priesthood. Instead, Friends compare their inner faith and feelings with the Bible and with the truths discerned by other Friends. They strongly seek consensus, both among Friends at their regular weekly meetings and at regularly scheduled meetings with Friends from other areas. In their day-to-day living, Quakers stress honesty, equality, simplicity, and peace.

In seventeenth-century England, Quakers not only refused to submit to the established religious authorities but also refused to submit to secular authorities. They would not participate in war, nor would they so much as take off their hats as a gesture of respect for rank, since they believed that all men and women were equal in the sight of God and should be so treated. George Fox wrote in his journal:

> When the Lord sent me into the world, he forbade me to put off my hat to any, high or low: and I was required to "thee" and "thou" [the familiar, rather than respectfully formal, manner of speech at that time] all men and women, without respect to rich or poor, great or small. And as I traveled up and down, . . . neither might I bow or scrape with my leg to any one. . . . Oh! the scorn, heat, and fury that arose! Oh! the blows, punchings, beatings, and imprisonments that we underwent for not putting off our hats to men! Some had their hats violently plucked off and thrown away, so that they quite lost them. The bad language and evil usage we received on this account

is hard to be expressed, besides the danger
we were sometimes in of losing our lives
for this matter.[4]

For refusing to bow to authority, the Quakers were
violently persecuted. Many went to jail.

Quakers in America

The Quakers sent their first messengers to America
in the 1650s, and George Fox himself visited Friends
there from 1671 to 1673. (By this time, the center of
Quakerism was already beginning to shift to
America. Today, half of the world's Quakers live in
the United States.) At the time of Fox's visit, most of
the Quakers in North America were living in colonies controlled by the religiously intolerant Puritans,
who found Quakerism monstrously offensive. In
Massachusetts, Puritan authorities executed four
Quaker missionaries. In the other colonies, treatment
of Quakers was less harsh, but rarely welcoming.

In the 1680s, however, the new colony of Pennsylvania—founded by the Quaker William Penn—
made a safe haven for Quakers. There, through the
rest of the colonial era, Quakers both prospered and
further developed their distinctive religion. Relations among various groups of Quakers became
clearly organized. Regulations governing everything from how meetings were to be conducted to
how children were to be educated were written
down and obeyed.

After the Revolutionary War, as a new government was established, the Quakers' grip on the political and social life of Pennsylvania slipped. As

pacifists, Quakers throughout the colonies had opposed the Revolutionary War. They declared themselves neutral and refused to support either side in the war in any way. They would not serve in armed forces, even if drafted, nor would they pay substitutes to serve for them. They would not pay fines for refusing to serve or even taxes levied to pay for the war—even if it meant going to jail. After the Revolutionary War, the victors pushed Quakers to the margins of civic life, even in Pennsylvania.

In addition, during this time disagreements were growing up among the Quakers themselves, distracting them from playing active roles in secular matters. First, in the late 1700s, dissenting members were purged from the ranks of Quakers. Then, in the early 1800s, the Friends broke apart into several separate organizations.

Even so, during this difficult time Quakers came to focus clearly and uncompromisingly on two lasting social concerns: a commitment to oppose war in all cases, and an opposition to slavery, which they concluded was immoral.

Even before the American Revolution, Quaker meetings from northern New England south to the Carolinas had condemned slavery and insisted that their members free any slaves they owned. In the early and mid-1800s, as the United States moved toward civil war over the issue, such Quakers as John Greenleaf Whittier and Lucretia Mott were among those most active in opposing slavery and helping runaway slaves to reach freedom. Much as they opposed slavery, however, the pacifist Quakers refused to participate in the Civil War, which ultimately ended the practice.

Quakers were central to the abolitionist movement in the mid-nineteenth century. Lucretia Mott and her husband James (fifth and sixth from left in the first row), were tireless abolitionists and belonged to the Society of Friends.

Meanwhile, through the 1800s and into the twentieth century, Quakers—like other Americans—fanned out westward across North America. Although Philadelphia has remained the main focal point for Quakerism, fully two thirds of U.S. Quakers now live west of the Appalachian Mountains.

Modern Quakers

Toward the end of the 1800s, a new, "liberal" consensus began to emerge among Quakers that helped heal the rifts of the past century and set an agenda for the century ahead. This consensus first emerged from Quaker schools and colleges, where learned Friends were seeking to reconcile their faith with the work of such modern scientists as Charles Darwin, whose theory of evolution challenged traditional interpretations of scripture.

The most influential American Quaker thinker of the first half of the twentieth century, Rufus Jones, a professor at Haverford College and a prolific writer, fused Quaker traditions with a clear-eyed view of the material world in a distinctive activist mysticism. Jones took the traditional Quaker rejection of church-bound sacraments to mean that *all* aspects of Quaker life were sacramental, that God's presence permeated His entire creation. Like the Shakers and Hasidim, Jones held that there were opportunities for communion with God in every act of everyday life. Furthermore, Jones upheld the Quaker tradition of gathering in groups as a uniquely rewarding and fruitful mystical experience—an inclusive mysticism that did not demand a suspension of rational, scientific thought, and a loving mysticism that inspired morally informed action.

At the core of the new liberal consensus was the sense that Quakers should be working to build a new society, both within the United States and abroad, that would be in harmony with Jesus' teachings that all people should love one another like brothers. Different Quakers have taken different approaches to this broad agenda. Some have focused on economic justice, seeking to reform or replace capitalism with a gentler system. Some have worked to achieve civil rights for blacks, women, and other disadvantaged groups. And many have worked to further the Friends' longstanding support of pacifism.

Peace Testimony in a Century of War

Individual Quakers responded in various ways to World War I. While all the groups of American Quaker meetings officially remained pacifist, more than two thirds of eligible Quaker men served in combat.[5]

Many Quakers felt that the unprecedented experience of "total war" in World War I demanded a fresh response from pacifists. In 1917 they created the American Friends Service Committee (AFSC), with Rufus Jones as its chairman. AFSC's goal has been to serve as a witness for peace in several interlinked ways: by helping conscientious objectors avoid military service, by providing humanitarian alternatives to military service, by helping to heal the damage caused by war, and by helping to build societies in which war is less likely to occur. Since its founding, AFSC has demonstrated its committment to peace:

Staunch advocates of peace, the American Friends Service Committee staged this anti-Vietnam War protest in 1973.

- During World War I, AFSC provided medical care and food for civilians on both sides of the conflict and helped with postwar reconstruction.

- During World War II, AFSC in conjunction with the U.S. government provided alternative service for conscientious objectors and participated in post war relief and reconstruction efforts. In 1947, AFSC shared the Nobel Peace Prize with British Quakers.

- During the Cold War arms race, AFSC worked for nuclear disarmament.

- During the wars in Korea and Vietnam, AFSC provided humanitarian aid to civilians and counseled thousands of draft-age Americans—Quaker and non-Quaker alike—about conscientious objection to military service.

In addition, AFSC has provided humanitarian aid and promoted peaceful resolution of conflicts in dozens of trouble spots around the world, from helping Jewish families to escape from Nazi Germany to feeding thousands during the 1992 conflict in Somalia.

Social Service: Making a Better World

Peace testimony, according to the Quakers, doesn't just mean opposing war. It also means working to build a world in which everyone can live and thrive as brothers and sisters. To this end, AFSC has involved itself in diverse efforts not directly related to war. Here, in their own words, is a sampling:

1921: Distributed milk, food, and medicine for famine relief in Russia

1929: Helped striking textile workers in North Carolina survive the winter

1931: Distributed food for 40,000 children of unemployed coal miners in Appalachia

1936: Helped sharecroppers in Arkansas improve farming methods; in West Virginia, founded first rural birth-control clinic in the United States

1943: Sent food to relieve severe famine in India

1958: Established home for parolees in Los Angeles, California, as part of continuing work on prison issues

1961: Sent young volunteers to work in developing countries; assisted in VISA program, forerunner to Peace Corps

1965: Helped place 7,000 black children in previously all-white southern schools; started long-term concern for school desegregation

1971: Provided daily meals to 16,000 malnourished children in Bangladesh

1972: Addressed immigration and unemployment issues on Mexico-U.S. border

1983: Supported Native Americans in their fishing and other treaty rights, in their efforts to end pollution of land and water, to establish better health for their people, and to publish more accurate school texts

1987: Addressed problems of homeless people in California, Hawaii, and Massachusetts

1989: Rebuilt health clinics in earthquake-devastated Armenia

1993: Established an information network for gay, lesbian, and transgender youth and those who work with them

1994: Shipped hay to midwestern farmers to feed their livestock after their crops were devastated by floods.[6]

The Quakers' public-service work has clearly gone well beyond simply reacting to war and other crises. In addition to their many hands-on, region-specific activities, they have maintained an active presence in Washington, D.C.—the Friends Committee on National Legislation (FCNL). Since 1943, FCNL has worked to promote legislation and other public policy that is in tune with Quaker values. FCNL lobbies and provides information to members of Congress and other public officials both face-to-face and through its publications. According to FCNL, over the years its "advocacy has touched a wide range of national issues, including: reconciliation among peoples and nations, opposition to militarism and proliferation of weapons, civil rights for all people, self-determination of Native Americans, democratic participation in public policy decisions, sustainable development in countries and areas where help is needed to meet people's basic needs, stewardship of resources to meet human needs and to care for the environment, economic and employment opportunities, more adequate housing, education, and health care, especially for the most vulnerable among us."[7]

Headlining its current (1995-1996) statement of legislative policy, FCNL describes the kind of world that American Quakers seek today:

We seek a world free of war and the threat of war
We seek a society with equity and justice for all
We seek a community where every person's
potential may be fulfilled
We seek an earth restored.[8]

It is a vision shared in one way or another by most communities of the faithful.

Old Order Amish

1. Quoted by Sue Bender, "Everyday Sacred: A Journey to the Amish," adapted from the book of the same name, *Utne Reader* (September-October, 1990), p. 94.
2. John A. Hostetler, *Amish Society*, 4th edition (Baltimore: Johns Hopkins, 1993), chart on p. 97 compiled from several sources.
3. Quoted in Randy-Michael Testa, *After the Fire: The Destruction of the Lancaster County Amish* (Hanover, NH: University Press of New England, 1992), p. 57.
4. Newspaper reportage quoted in Testa, p. 160.

Shakers

1. Quoted (with no citation, except "1966") by Steven J. Stein in *The Shaker Experience in America: A History of the United Society of Believers* (New Haven, CT: Yale University Press, 1992), p. xiii.
2. Cited in Stein, p. 27. The only record of Ann Lee's sayings is what her followers remembered and wrote down many years later.
3. Shaker biography of Ann Lee, quoted in Edward Rice, *American Saints and Seers: American-Born Religions and*

the Genius Behind Them (New York: Four Winds Press, 1982), p. 17.

4. Quoted in Stein, p. 27.
5. Quoted in Rice, p. 44.
6. Stein, p. 126.
7. Stein, pp. 203, 243.
8. Quoted in Stein, p. 349.
9. Republication of 1953 edition of Edward Deming Andrews, *The People Called Shakers* (New York: Dover, 1963), pp. 126-127.

Mormons

1. The Reverend T. De Witt Talmage, quoted in Leonard J. Arrington and Davis Bitton, *The Mormon Experience: A History of the Latter-day Saints*, 2nd ed. (Urbana: University of Illinois Press, 1992), p. 161.
2. Account later written by Joseph Smith, quoted in Edward Rice, *American Saints and Seers: American-Born Religions and the Genius Behind Them* (New York: Four Winds Press, 1982), p. 49.
3. Quoted in Arrington and Bitton, p. 44.
4. Letter dated 1843 from Charlotte Haven, a Mormon at Nauvoo, to her family, quoted in Arrington and Bitton, p. 70.
5. Sarah M. Kimball, writing in the 1880s, quoted in Arrington and Bitton, p. 222.
6. Quoted in Arrington and Bitton, p. 183.
7. Quoted in Arrington and Bitton, p. 122.
8. Official statement by First President in 1969, quoted in Arrington and Bitton, p. 322.
9. Quoted in Arrington and Bitton, p. 324.
10. Quoted in Arrington and Bitton, p. 228.
11. Quoted in Robert Gottlieb and Peter Wiley, *America's Saints: The Rise of Mormon Power* (New York: G.P. Putnam's Sons, 1984), p. 210.
12. Quoted in Arrington and Bitton, p. 237.

13. Sonia Johnson, *From Housewife to Heretic* (Garden City, NY: Doubleday, 1981), p. 118.
14. Johnson, p. 15.

Catholic Workers

1. From *The Catholic Worker* (April 1953), excerpted in *By Little and By Little: The Selected Writings of Dorothy Day* (New York: Knopf, 1983), p. 111.
2. From *The Long Loneliness: An Autobiography* (1952), excerpted in *By Little and By Little*, p. 39.
3. Quoted by Robert Ellsberg in his introduction to *By Little and By Little*, p. xxii.
4. Quoted in Mel Piehl, *Breaking Bread: The Catholic Worker and the Origin of Catholic Radicalism in America* (Philadelphia: Temple University Press, 1982), p. 57.
5. From *The Long Loneliness*, excerpted in *By Little and By Little*, p. 44.
6. Dorothy Day, quoting Peter Maurin, from *The Catholic Worker* (June 1949), excerpted in *By Little and By Little*, p. 126.
7. From *The Long Loneliness*, excerpted in *By Little and By Little*, p. 240.
8. From *The Long Loneliness*, excerpted in *By Little and By Little*, p. 235.
9. From *The Catholic Worker* (December 1945), excerpted in *By Little and By Little*, p. 94.
10. From *The Catholic Worker* (February and May 1934), excerpted in *By Little and By Little*, pp. 60, 61.
11. From *The Catholic Worker* (December 1936), excerpted in *By Little and By Little*, p. 79.
12. From *The Long Loneliness*, excerpted in *By Little and By Little*, p. 236.
13. Piehl, p. 67.
14. From *The Catholic Worker* (March-April 1975), excerpted in *By Little and By Little*, p. 354.

15. From *The Catholic Worker* (January 1942), excerpted in *By Little and By Little*, p. 262.
16. From *The Catholic Worker* (July-August 1963), excerpted in *By Little and By Little*, p. 328.
17. From *The Catholic Worker* (January 1972), excerpted in *By Little and By Little*, p. 252.
18. Quoted in Piehl, p. 104.
19. From *On Pilgrimage* (1948), excerpted in *By Little and By Little*, p. 213.
20. From *The Long Loneliness*, excerpted in *By Little and By Little*, pp. 362-363.

Nation of Islam

1. Quoted in Clifton E. Marsh, *From Black Muslims to Muslims: The Transition from Separatism to Islam, 1930-1980* (Metuchen, NJ: Scarecrow Press, 1984), p. 75.
2. Quoted in Marshall Frady, "The Children of Malcolm," *New Yorker*, October 12, 1992, p. 70.
3. Quoted in Frady, p. 72.
4. Quoted in Frady, p. 72.
5. Quoted in Frady, p. 72.
6. From *Muhammad Speaks*, quoted in Adolph Reed, Jr., "The Rise of Louis Farrakhan," *The Nation*, January 21, 1991.
7. Nation of Islam World Wide Web page, quoted in *The New York Times*, October 22, 1995.
8. *The New York Times*, October 15, 1995.
9. *The New York Times*, October 17, 1995.
10. *The New York Times*, May 2, 1993.
11. *The New York Times*, March 3, 1994.
12. Major R. Owens, on Farrakhan's appeal, quoted in *The New York Times*, March 5, 1994.

Lubavitcher Hasidim

1. Quoted in Lis Harris, "Holy Days—I," *New Yorker*, September 16, 1985.

2. Quoted in Harris.
3. Quoted in Harris.
4. Quoted in Lynn Davidman and Janet Stocks, "Varieties of Fundamentalist Experience: Lubavitch Hasidic and Fundamentalist Christian Approaches to Family Life," in *New World Hasidim: Ethnographic Studies of Hasidic Jews in America*, edited by Janet S. Belcove-Shalin (Albany: State University of New York Press, 1995), p. 115.
5. Publication dated 1970, quoted in Ellen Koskoff, "The Language of the Heart: Music in Lubavitcher Life," in *New World Hasidim*, p. 96.
6. *The New York Times*, January 29, 1993.
7. *The New York Times*, January 28, 1996.
8. Koskoff, p. 105.
9. *The New York Times*, June 13, 1994.

Quakers

1. From policy statement printed in FCNL's *Washington Newsletter*, December 1994.
2. Margaret Fell, quoted in Hugh Barbour and J. William Frost, *The Quakers* (New York: Greenwood, 1988), p. 27.
3. Fox's 1652 *Epistles*, quoted in Barbour and Frost, p. 39.
4. Quoted in William James, *The Varieties of Religious Experience* (New York: New American Library), p. 231.
5. Barbour and Frost, p. 251.
6. Excerpted from "Introduction to the American Friends Service Committee," a brochure published in October 1994 by AFSC, Philadelphia.
7. "What Is FCNL?" undated publication of FCNL, Washington, D.C.
8. FCNL's *Washington Newsletter*, December 1994.

INDEX

Page numbers in *italics* refer to illustrations.

Alfred, Maine, 38
Allah, 72, 80
American Friends Service Committee (AFSC), 108, *109*, 110
Amish, 15-26
    baptism and, 18
    childhood of, 19, 20, *21*, 22
    education and, 20, 22
    family life of, 19-20
    farming and, *14*, 17-18, 23, 25, 26
    marriage and, 22-23
    pacifism and, 17

Amish *(continued)*
    population of, 23
    religion of, 16, 18, 20
    self-government by, 16
    shunning and, 18-19
    tourism and, 25-26
    women, 19, 20
Amman, Jacob, 16
Anabaptists, 15-16, 29
Andrews, Edward Deming, 39
Architecture, Shaker, 37-38

Baal Shem Tov (Rabbi Israel ben Eliezer), 87
Baptism, Amish, 18
Benson, Ezra Taft, 52

Birth control, 92
Black Mormons, 50
Black Muslims (*see*
   Nation of Islam)
Black nationalism, 76-
   77
Black Panthers, 78
Black separatism, 77-
   78
Boggs, Lilburn W., 45
Book of Mormon, 43, 44

Canterbury, New
   Hampshire, 38
Catholic Worker, The
   (newspaper), 61, *62*,
   63, 64
Catholic Worker move-
   ment, 56-69
      Houses of Hospi-
         tality, 61, 65-66,
         69
      newspaper of, 61,
         62, 63, 64
      pacifism and, 56-
         69
      three-point pro-
         gram of, 60
      volunteers, 65
Celibacy, Shaker, 33, 37
Chavez, Cesar, 64
Chavis, Benjamin, 79
Childhood, Amish, 19-
   20, *21*, 22

Church of Jesus Christ
   of Latter-day Saints
   (*see* Mormons)
Civil-rights movement,
   50, 66
Civil War, 105
Communists, 58, 64
Conscientious objec-
   tion, 110
Crown Heights, New
   York, 88, 92, 94-95,
   96, 97

Darrow, David, 32
Darwin, Charles, 107
Day, Dorothy, 56, 58-61,
   63-66, *67*, 68-69
Dress
      of Lubavitcher
         Hasidim, *86*
      of Shakers, 37

Education
      Amish, 20, 22
      Mormon, 51
Equal Rights Amend-
   ment (ERA), 53

Family life
      Amish, 19-20
      Shaker, 33, 34
Farad, Wali, 71-72, 80
Farming, Amish and,
   14, 17-18, 23, 25, 26

Farrakhan, Louis, 71, 76, 78-80
Feminine aspect of God, 29-30, 32
Fox, George, 100, 102-104
Friends Committee on National Legislation (FCNL), 112-113
Fruit of Islam, 78

Garvey, Marcus, 77
Great Basin, 45
Great Depression, 63, 66
Great Salt Lake, 46

Hancock, Massachusetts, *34*, 37, 38
Hasidim (*see* Lubavitcher Hasidim)
Holocaust, 85, 88, 92, 97, 99
Houses of Hospitality, 61, 65-66, 69

Inventions, Shaker, 35
Islam, 71, 80, *81*, 82-83

Jackson, Jesse, 79
Johnson, Sonia, 53, *54*, 55
Jones, Rufus, 107, 108

King, Martin Luther, Jr., 73

Lancaster, Pennsylvania, 15, 23, 25, 26
Lee, Ann, 27, 29, 30, 32, 35, 36
Lee, William, 29, 30
Lubavitcher Hasidim, 85-99
    dress of, *86*
    less-observant Jews and, 98-99
    marriage and, 90-91
    population of, 85, 95
    rebbes, 87-88, 92, *93*, 94, 97-98
    religion of, 88-89

Malcolm X, 71, 73-74, *75*, 76, 78
Manifesto (Mormon), 48
Marriage
    Amish, 22-23
    Lubavitcher Hasidim, 90-91
    Mormon, 46, 48, 49
    Shaker, 33
Maurin, Peter, 58-61, 64, 66, 68
Meacham, Joseph, 30, 32

Mecca, 74
Mennonite church, 16
Merton, Thomas, 27
Messiah, 97-98
Million Man March
(1995), 79-80
Missionaries
Mormon, 50
Shaker, 29, 30
Mitzvot, 88-90
Mormons, 41-55
black, 50
economic solidar-
ity of, 49
education and, 51
missionaries, 50
persecution and
violence
against, 44-45
polygamy and, 46
48, 49
population of, 46
religion of, 43-44
women, 41, 46, 50-
53, 54, 55
Moroni, 43, 44
Mother Ann's Work, 36-
37
Mott, James, *106*
Mott, Lucretia, 105,
106
Moussia, Chaya, 88
Muhammad, Elijah
(Elijah Poole), 71-74,
78, 80

Muhammad, W. Deen,
78

Nation of Islam, 71-84
black separatism
and, 77-78
central belief of, 72
converts to, 72-73
Farrakhan and, 71,
76, 78-80
Islam and, 80, 82-83
Malcolm X and,
71, 73-74, *75*, 76
membership of,
73, 78, 83
Native Americans, 43,
111-112
Nauvoo, Illinois, 45
New Lebanon, New
York, 32, 38
Niskeyuna, 29
Nuclear arms race, 66,
110

Old Order Amish (*see*
Amish)

Pacifism
Amish and, 17
Catholic Worker
movement and,
56-69
Quakers and, 105,
108, *109*, 110
Shakers and, 29, 36

Penn, William, 104
People Called Shakers, The
(Andrews), 39
Persecution
of Mormons, 44-45
of Quakers, 103-104
Polygamy, 46, 48, 49
Population
Amish, 23
Lubavitcher
Hasidim, 85, 95
Mormons, 46
Shaker, 37
Puritans, 104

Quakers, 100-113
early, 100, *101*, 102-
104
modern, 107-108
pacifism and, 105,
108, *109*, 110
persecution of, 103-
104
public-service
work of, 110-113
slavery and, 105

Radical Catholicism,
60
Rebbes, 87-88, 92, *93*,
94, 97-98
Religion
Amish, 16, 18, 20
Lubavitcher
Hasidim, 88-89

Religion *(continued)*
Mormon, 43-44
Quaker, 102-103
Shaker, 27, 29-30,
31, 32-33, 35-36
Religious persecution,
16, 26, 27
Revolutionary War, 29,
104, 105
Ritual bath (*mikvah*), 91-
92

Sabbath, 89
Sabbathday Lake,
Maine, 38
Schneerson, Menachem
Mendel, 88, *93*, 94,
97-99
Schneersohn, Yosef, 88,
92
Shakers, 27-40
architecture of, 37-
38
dress of, 37
family life of, 33,
34
furniture of, *28*, 38-
40
inventions by, 35
marriage and, 33
missionaries, 29,
30
pacifism and, 29,
36
population of, 37

Shakers *(continued)*
   religion of, 27, 29-
     30, *31*, 32-33, 35-
     36
   women, 32, 33, 35
Shunning, 18-19
Smith, Emma, 46
Smith, Joseph, 41, 42-
   46
Society of Friends *(see*
   Quakers)

Tourism, Amish and,
   25-26
Tree of Life drawings,
   37

United Farmworkers
   Union, 64
United Society of Believ-
   ers in Christ's Second
   Appearing *(see* Shakers)
Universal Negro Im-
   provement Associa-
   tion, 77
University of Deseret,
   51

Vietnam War, 66
Voting rights, 51

Watervliet, New York, 38
Whittaker, James, 29, 30,
   32
Whittier, John Greenleaf,
   105
Women
   Amish, 19, 20
   Hasidic, 90-92
   Islam and, 82-83
   Mormon, 41, 46,
     50-53, *54*, 55
   Shaker, 32, 33, 35
Women's movement, 52,
   53
Woodruff, Wilford,
   48
World Community of
   Al-Islam in the West,
   78
Wright, Lucy, 32

Yacub, 72
Young, Brigham, 45, *47*,
   49, 51